Enter Laughing

A COMEDY IN TWO ACTS

by

Joseph Stein

Adapted from the novel
by Carl Reiner

SAMUEL
FR
FOU
New York Holly
SAMUELF

D1115387

ENTER LAUGHING, a comedy by Joseph Stein, based on the novel by Carl Reiner, under the direction of Gene Saks, was presented by Morton Gottlieb at Henry Miller's Theatre, N.Y.C., March 13, 1963.

CHARACTERS

(In Order Of Their Appearance)

MR. FOREMAN	Irving Jacobson
DAVID KOLOWITZ	Alan Arkin
MARVIN	Michael J. Pollard
MISS B.	Meg Myles
PIKE	Charles Randall
DON BAXTER	Pierre Epstein
DON DARWIN	Walt Wanderman
MARLOWE	Alan Mowbray
ANGELA	Vivian Blaine
MOTHER	Sylvia Sidney
FATHER	Marty Greene
WANDA	Barbara Dana
WAITER	Shimen Ruskin
ROGER	Monroe Arnold
LAWYER	Tom Gorman

New York

The Mid-1930's

Late Spring

There will be one intermission.

3

ENTER LAUGHING

ACT ONE

Scene 1

Time: Summer, the mid-thirties.

Place: New York City.

Scene: A small, one-room, cluttered machine shop; NRA sign on wall.

At Rise: MR. FOREMAN, a middle-aged, harried Jewish man, is seated at D.S. bench, working at a machine. The phone rings. He rises, crosses to S.R. of U.S. bench.

FOREMAN. *(into phone)* Hello? ... Yes, this is Foreman Machines, who you want? ... Mr. Kolowitz. Mr. Kolowitz? You mean David. He ain't here. He's delivering.... Call back when he's here. *(Hangs up, abruptly. Back to D.S. bench and works, talks to self.)* Mr. Kolowitz! Every peanut in America is a mister; President Roosevelt is a mister, Albert Einstein is a mister and my foolish delivery boy is also a mister—America! *(Phone rings. Shouts at phone on second ring.)* What is it? What? *(Rises, picks up phone.)* Hello?

What? I told you he's delivering. I should tell him *who's* calling? Wanda? What kind name is Wanda? Are you a Jewish girl? ... All right. I'll tell him when he comes. *(Hangs up, to self.)* Mixed up with girls already.... *(Sits. Gets tag from drawer of D.S. table.)* A nothing, fourteen dollars and fifty cents a week, mixed up with girls.... *(Tying tag on machine.)* She ain't Jewish! ... Ah, why should I worry; let his father worry.... Everything's a *mister! (Shakes head, disbelievingly.)* America!

(DAVID enters U.L., a tall, nice-looking boy.)

DAVID. They paid by check, Mr. Foreman. Eighteen-fifty! *(Puts check on table. Crosses below table to S.R. wall.)*

FOREMAN. *(Takes check, formally, watches him cross, then speaks.)* Thank you, *Mr.* Kolowitz.

DAVID. *(Taking of jacket, hangs it on hook on S.R. wall.)* What?

FOREMAN. Tell me, David, you mixed up with a girl; she's not Jewish?

DAVID. *(smiling)* What?

FOREMAN. A girl called. She said she's Jewish, but she didn't sound Jewish.

DAVID. You *asked* her?

FOREMAN. *(rising S.R. of stool)* David, you listen to me. Don't get mixed up with girls yet. You're a young boy, a nothing.... I'm going to lunch. *(Takes off apron as he crosses U.S. to hook on C. wall S.R. of shelves. Hangs up apron; gets coat.)*

DAVID. *(Crosses to R. of table.)* What was her name?

FOREMAN. *(picking up check from table)* She told me, but I

forgot—Gertrude, I think.

DAVID. Wanda?

FOREMAN. That's right, Wanda. *(Crosses U.S. to door.)* If anybody calls, write it down. Always write down the name. *(Exits U.L., upstage of second portal.)*

DAVID. *(Waits for a few seconds, till FOREMAN is definitely gone; goes to phone.)* Operator, Tremont eight-oh-six-seven.

(MARVIN enters. MARVIN is DAVID'S age; he is not too good-looking, and a little timid, unsure of himself. He admires DAVID, just this side of hero worship. He carries his lunch, wrapped in a newspaper.)

DAVID. Hi, Marv.

MARVIN. Hi. *(Crossing to L. of table, gets chair from U.L., moves it to L. of table. Sits and eats.)*

DAVID. I'm calling Wanda. *(into phone)* Hello, Wanda? Did you call me? ... He told me.... Yeah, Marvin just came down. He's having his lunch.... Saturday night? Gee, I'd love to, Wanda, only my mother and father are visiting some relatives in Flatbush, and I've got to mind my stupid kid sister. Who's giving the dance? ... Well, listen, Wanda, maybe after the dance, you and me could get together and have a little tete-a-tete. *(imitating Ronald Coleman)* "It will be a far, far better thing that you and I will do on Saturday night than has ever been done before." ... Yes, Ronald Colman, that's right! ... Goodbye. *(Hangs up and moves chair from U.R. to S.R. of table.)*

MARVIN. Boy, the way you do those imitations. You're

great, you know that, Dave?

*(DAVID then goes into a Louis Armstrong routine in midst of which
        MARVIN says: "Louis Armstrong." At end of it he takes rag
        from bench and dabs face.)*

MARVIN. Great!

DAVID. I know. *(He sits R. of table.)*

MARVIN. And the way you talk to girls. Boy, I wish I had
a steady girl, like you.

DAVID. You do?

MARVIN. I sure do. A steady girl, boy.

DAVID. I'll tell you, Marv, even though I got a steady
girl, I think about other girls.

MARVIN. You do?

DAVID. Yeah, a lot. Do you think about girls a lot?

MARVIN. Me? I don't know what you mean by a lot.
Sometimes I think about other things.

DAVID. Like what?

MARVIN. *(Considers.)* Oh, you know, other things —
food.

DAVID. *(Rises. Crosses L. below table, above it, then to S.R. of
it.)* I think about girls a lot. I admit it. Like if I'm walking
down the street, I see a girl swinging along—you know the
way they do when they're walking, the way they walk.

MARVIN. Yeah —

DAVID. *(crossing U.S. and D.S.)* Sometimes I go two, three
blocks out of my way, just to watch the way they walk.

MARVIN. Me, too.

DAVID. *(U.S.C. of table)* I think about it a lot. Like there's
this bookkeeper at the LaTesh Hat Company. Her name

is Miss B., she's the most zaftig thing you ever saw, Marve, I mean it —

MARVIN. Her name is Miss B.?

DAVID. *(at R. of S.R. chair)* That's what they call her. Anyway, she'd drive you crazy if her name was Irving.

MARVIN. I thought you're crazy about Wanda.

DAVID. I am. I'm crazy about Wanda. And I'm crazy about Miss B. And I'm crazy about strange girls on the street. Sometimes I think I'm a sex maniac.

MARVIN. Yeah, me too.

DAVID. *(crossing R. to U.R., then D.S.)* Only one thing, I talk a lot, but I don't do anything. *(Sits, chair R. of table.)* I'm a big talker.

MARVIN. Me, too.

DAVID. *(Rises, above table.)* Another thing. What am I doing in this crummy job? I mean, okay, just for a while, but Mr. Foreman thinks I want to learn the business — what do I want to be a machinest on ladies hats for? *(Picks up two files from table.)*

MARVIN. Then don't.

DAVID. Okay, then why don't I tell him? He keeps saying, "You'll work hard, be a good machinist," and I say, "Sure, Mr. Foreman...."

MARVIN. Do you want an apple?

DAVID. No. *(drumming on shelves with files)* And my parents, they want me to be a druggist. *(Drums.)* They want me to register in night school for September, to be a druggist. *(Drums.)* I don't want to be a druggist.

MARVIN. Then why don't you tell them?

DAVID. *(drumming)* I did tell them. I kind of told them. So they say, "What do you want to be? You can't be a nothing. Everyone calls me a nothing. *(Throws files in tray on table. Sits S.R. of table.)*

MARVIN. You know, I wouldn't mind being a druggist.

DAVID. You? You'd poison the whole neighborhood. *(Rises to U.S.C. of table.)* The thing is, I want to be something. Something so people will say, "There goes Dave Kolowitz, the something."

MARVIN. What's the matter with, "There goes the druggist?"

DAVID. *(Crosses R.)* Naah.

MARVIN. *(ofering apple)* You sure you don't want an apple?

DAVID. *(Crosses to above table.)* What's with you and the apple? What's it got, worms or something? *(Crosses L. above table, to L. of table.)* You know, if I had any guts, I'd pack up and go to Panama or someplace.

MARVIN. Why don't you?

DAVID. *(at S.L.; shouts)* Because I have to mind my stupid kid sister Saturday night, that's why.

MARVIN. *(Rises, steps L. to DAVID with apple.)* Okay, you don't have to bite my head off.

DAVID. *(pause)* Give me the apple.

MARVIN. I bit it already.

DAVID. What are you giving me an apple for and then eating it yourself?

MARVIN. It ain't my fault you don't know what you want to be.

DAVID. Did I say I don't know what I want to be? I know what I want to be.

MARVIN. Yeah — a something!

DAVID. *(Crosses R. below table, to R. of table.)* No. I'll tell you what I want to be. I want to be an actor.

MARVIN. An *actor?*

DAVID. *(Crosses D.S.R. of table.)* Sure. Why not? An actor! *(Faces audience, poses.)*

MARVIN. You know something? You'd be great!

DAVID. I know. But you can't just be an actor. You can't just go around and tell people — "Hello, I'm an actor!"

MARVIN. *(crossing R. to DAVID)* Hey, I saw this ad in today's paper. I saw it yesterday, too. I saw it both days.

DAVID. An ad? For what?

MARVIN. For actors.

DAVID. For actors?

MARVIN. For actors.

DAVID. You're crazy! *(Goes U.S., takes newspaper from shelf on C. wall.)*

MARVIN. *(Crosses L. of table, to above it, taking paper from DAVID, finds ad.)* It's here, right here in the paper. I saw it yesterday; I saw it today.... Here. When I saw it I even thought about you.

DAVID. *(Reads; U.S. of S.R. chair.)* "Marlowe Theatre and School for Dramatic Arts ... Scholarships for Promising Young Actors..."

MARVIN. *(at S.L. of DAVID)* Just do your Ronald Coleman or your Humphrey Bogart.

DAVID. "Learn to act before audiences."

MARVIN. No kidding, you're a cinch.

(DAVID crosses S.R. MARVIN follows.)

DAVID. They'll see applicants at six o'clock.

MARVIN. What do you say, will you go?

DAVID. Sure. Why not?

MARVIN. Bet you a dime you don't.

DAVID. It's a bet.

(They shake hands.)

MARVIN. *(Gets apple from table.)* Here. I only took one bite.

DAVID. Thanks. Wait a second. I can't make it, though. I don't get out of here till six o'clock —

MARVIN. Listen, you don't want to be a machinist or a druggist all your life?

DAVID. Besides, I got to be home tonight. What will I tell my mother?

MARVIN. Okay, okay, you lose; give me the dime.

FOREMAN. *(Enters, crossing to U.S. of D.S. table.)* You here again? *(Takes off coat and hangs it on hook, S.L. of shelves.)*

(DAVID crosses U.R.)

MARVIN. I was just leaving, Mr. Foreman. *(Crosses L. below table; picks up lunch. Throws apple in waste basket under shelf on C. wall.)*

FOREMAN. Pick up your dirt, and go back to your shop. *(Hangs up hat.)*

MARVIN. Sure, Mr. Foreman. *(Picks up bag, etc., throws in basket under U.S. table. Takes chair from L. of table to D.S. of door.)*

FOREMAN. Anybody call?

DAVID. *(Takes chair R. of table to U.R.)* No, Mr. Foreman.

FOREMAN. *(Crosses to sit U.C. above table.)* I want you to deliver this machine to LaTesh Hats.

(MARVIN is at door.)

DAVID. LaTesh Hats? *(Makes delighted face at MARVIN. Goes for jacket on S.R. wall.)*

FOREMAN. Right away.

DAVID. Sure, Mr. Foreman — *(Looks at MARVIN. Crosses L. to FOREMAN.)* Oh, and Mr. Foreman, I'm going to have to leave about an hour early tonight. *(Puts jacket on.)*

(MARVIN listens.)

FOREMAN. Why?

DAVID. I have to pick up something for my father. At six o'clock.

FOREMAN. What do you have to pick up for your father?

DAVID. My mother — *(Hesitates.)* She's visiting my aunt.

FOREMAN. All right, all right —

MARVIN. Here's the dime I owe you, Dave. *(Throws imaginary dime to DAVID.)*

(DAVID catches it, and puts it in his pocket.)

FOREMAN. *(rising, crossing L. to MARVIN)* You still here?

MARVIN. No. I just left. *(He exits.)*

FOREMAN. I wish he worked for me so I could fire him! LaTesh Hats. And don't forget the receipt.

DAVID. Okay, Mr. Foreman. *(Exits with machine, crossing above table.)*

ACT ONE

Scene 2

Scene: The office of LaTesh Hat Company. It contains a desk, a filing cabinet, hat boxes. MISS B., a luscious blonde in her early twenties, is seated at desk. She is interrupted by a VOICE from D.S.L.

VOICE. Miss B.

MISS B. Yes?

VOICE. Will you bring me the Bon Marche order?

MISS B. Okay, Mr. Firestein. *(Rises, opens filing cabinet drawer, bends over with her back to the audience.)*

DAVID. *(Enters from S.R., stops at C. He crosses L. and speaks.)* Miss B. —

MISS B. *(straightening up.)* Well, hello, David.

DAVID. Hello, Miss B.

MISS B. *(Crosses to S.L. of desk.)* I see you brought our machine back.

DAVID. *(Crosses to R. of desk. Puts machine on desk.)* That was my practical reason for coming. But I must confess that I would welcome any reason for coming into your presence.

MISS B. My, what a handsome speech.

DAVID. I suppose you mean by that, that only my speech is handsome.

Miss B. Well, as long as your fishing for a compliment, I'll bite. I think you're quite a handsome boy, too.

David. Thank you. But look who's talking. As long as we're getting slightly more personal, Miss B., do you mind if I try to guess what the B. stands for?

Miss B. *(leaning across desk to him)* No.

David. Betty?

Miss B. No.

David. Beatrice?

Miss B. No.   David. Bernie?

(MISS B. shakes her head, chuckling.)

David. I give up. What?

Miss B. Laura.

David. Laura? With a B?

Miss B. The B. is Miss Burke. Laura Burke.

David. Laura — Laura — Laura Burke! One look at you and my heart doth jerk.

Miss B. *(amused and pleased with him)* You know, David, you sound very different today. You certainly don't talk like a delivery boy from Foreman's Machine Shop.

David. *(crossing R. a few steps)* That's just a temporary ocupation, Miss B. — Laura.

Miss B. *(She crosses to R. of desk.)* Oh? And what are your plans for the future?

David. My plans are to become an actor.

Miss B. An Actor?

David. Yeah. Why not? An actor.

Miss B. That's very exciting, David. But how do you know you can act? Have you ever acted before?

DAVID. Well, not professionally. Semi-professionally, you might say. *(a la Ronald Colman)* Ah, Laura, Laura — it is a far, far better thing that I do than I have ever done.

MISS B. *(impressed)* That sounds just like Douglas Fairbanks, Junior.

DAVID. No, it's Ronald Colman. Gee, I can do both of them!

MISS B. Well, that certainly is exciting.

DAVID. In fact, I'm going for an acting part today.

MISS B. Are you really? I'd love to hear all about it.

DAVID. I'd love to tell you about it. May I suggest, how about lunch tomorrow?

MISS B. *(crossing below him to R. of him)* Lunch tomorrow? I don't know ...

DAVID. Oh — are you by any chance going steady?

MISS B. Not what you'd call steady. I have a gentleman friend. But we haven't exchanged rings or anything as final as that.

DAVID. *(Crosses R. to her.)* In that case, if he's a true gentleman and a true friend, he wouldn't be offended if you shared a cornbeef sandwich with another friend.

MISS B. Of course not.

DAVID. *(seductively)* And even a pickle!

MISS B. *(Laughs.)* You're certainly a cute boy.

VOICE. Miss B.! Will you come in here, please?

MISS B. *(Crosses L. to chair L. of desk.)* Right away, Mr. Firestein. *(to DAVID)* Very well. I'll meet you at twelve, tomorrow.

DAVID. *(happily backing off R. theatrically)* I'm delighted, Laura....

ROGER. *(entering)* Miss B., will you file this..... *(notices*

DAVID) Hey, don't you know by now, deliveries in the back...

Miss B. You shouldn't talk to him like that, Roger. Some day, you'll have to pay to see him.

ROGER. Why?

Miss B. He's going to be an actor.

ROGER. *(contemptuous)* An actor?

DAVID. *(theatrically)* Thank you, Miss B. *(Starts to exit.)*

ROGER. Hey! Until you're an actor .... deliveries in the back!

DIMOUT

ACT ONE

Scene 3

*Scene: Stage of Marlowe Theatre .... Two young men standing
around, waiting, as DAVID enters.... He joins them....
PIKE enters, carrying clipboard....*

PIKE. Any more here? Just you three? *(Looks at clipboard.)* All right. What's your name?

DON BAXTER. *(stepping forward)* Don Baxter.

PIKE. You?

DON DARWIN. *(stepping forward)* Don Darwin.

PIKE. Okay. You?

DAVID. *(stepping forward)* Don ... er ... R.

PIKE. Don R. what?

DAVID. Ron — uh .. no ... Don Colman.

PIKE. Which is it?

DAVID. Both. Don Ron Colman ... Don *R.* Colman!

PIKE. Okay. Wait in the wings, Dons.

DAVID. Where, sir?

PIKE. In the wings. Out there!

(MARLOWE enters, counting money.)

PIKE. Mr. Marlowe.

MARLOWE. *(waving him off)* Eight-seventy...eight-eighty ...eight-eighty-one...eight-eighty-two.... Is this it, Pike?

PIKE. That's it.

MARLOWE. *(handling coins)* These are the entire receipts from last night's performance?

PIKE. That's it.

MARLOWE. I counted more than thirty people in the audience.

PIKE. A lot of them just put a dime in the plate, or nothing. Some just came in to get out of the rain.

MARLOWE. *(Opening a bottle of liquor, he puts a straw in it and sips through the following:)* That I've descended to this! Put a dime in the plate and see Harrison Marlowe! ... Eight dollars and eighty-two cents! Two cents? Some monster actually paid two cents for a three-act play.... Less than a penny an act! And the world wonders why I drink! Anyone show up?

PIKE. Three of them; listen to this: Don Baxter, Don Darwin, and Don Colman.

MARLOWE. Oh God! *(He again sips from bottle; puts bottle, with straw, into inside breast-pocket.)* Oh, Don! .....

(PIKE turns.)

MARLOWE. Where is my darling daughter?

PIKE. I don't know. She said she'd be...

ANGELA. *(entering)* Daddy! There are three new boys waiting out there.

MARLOWE. I know. Any of them look like anything?

ANGELA. Why?

MARLOWE. One of them will be your new leading man.

ANGELA. New leading ... what happened to Barry Holloway?

MARLOWE. I fired him.

ANGELA. How could you do that? ... He was wonderful.... He was my height.... Why?

MARLOWE. Because he quit. The idiot wanted to be paid.

ANGELA. Oh! Well, if you don't mind, *I'll* pick my own leading man this time..

MARLOWE. May I remind you that this is my theatre and I pick the actors.

ANGELA. You pick them, but *I* Have to perform with them. You don't care what they look like —. All you care about is how much money you can squeeze out of them.

MARLOWE. All right, all right! *(to PIKE)* Let's take a look at the creatures.

PIKE. *(calling)* All right, gentlemen....

(They enter)

PIKE. This is Mr. Marlowe....

MARLOWE. *(He examines them. To himself:)* To be or not to be is going to be a helluva question. *(to PIKE)* Tell them to wait out there.

PIKE. Will you wait out there?

DAVID. In the wings?

PIKE. Yes, in the wings.

(They start off.)

ANGELA. *(stopping them)* Just a moment, please. If I may, daddy...

(The boys stop. ANGELA walks up and down, examining boys.)

ANGELA. *(going down the line)* Have you had much experience?

DON BAXTER. Doing what?

ANGELA. Thank you. *(to DAN DARWIN)* How old are you?

DON DARWIN. *(bewildered)* I'm going to be 27.

ANGELA. Oh, yes — I'm sure you will be! *(to DAVID)* Hello.

DAVID. *(shyly)* Hello.

MARLOWE. Are you quite through?

ANGELA. I think so. Yes.

MARLOWE. Pike, tell them again.

PIKE. Wait out there.

(They start to exit.)

ANGELA. Daddy, let's have the cute one.

MARLOWE. Which one is the cute one?

ANGELA. The one who was looking at me..... The one in the red jacket.

MARLOWE. *(to PIKE)* Bring back James Monroe. *(He takes a sip from his inside breast-pocket.)*

PIKE. *(calling)* Don Colman! *(pause — no answer)* Don Colman!

DAVID. *(off stage)* Oh.... Me!! *(He comes back on-stage.*

MARLOWE. *(to DAVID as he enters)* Have you ever acted before, boy?

DAVID. Where, sir?

MARLOWE. In a play, boy.

DAVID. Well, not in a play exactly.

MARLOWE. In what then, exactly?

DAVID. Well, at this thing I sang 'The Isle of Capri', and I did my impersonations of Edward G. Robinson and Ronald Colman...

MARLOWE. At what *thing* did you do... these *things?*

DAVID. On Senior Day... *(pause)* ...in James Monroe High School... *(Indicates back of jacket.)*

(MARLOWE stares at him.)

DAVID. *(continuing)* ...That's in the Bronx.

MARLOWE. Wonderful! *(He takes a sip through straw from hidden bottle.)* Well, let's see one of the other —

ANGELA. *(walking up to them)* Perhaps we should hear Mister Monroe read.

DAVID. *(interjecting)* Colman!

ANGELA. He may have a natural talent.

MARLOWE. *(staring at her)* You think so!

ANGELA. Daddy, we'll never know unless we...

MARLOWE. *(breaking in; to PIKE)* Let him have the script.

(PIKE hands the script to DAVID.)

MARLOWE. Read the part of Jeff Heming. Mr. Pike will cue you.

DAVID. He'll do what, sir?

MARLOWE. He'll cue you. You know what that means?

DAVID. Er...; you mean he'll cue me wherever I have to be cued.

MARLOWE. Yes, now — take it from Jeff's entrance. They're serving tea, and Harriet says, 'That must be Jeff now.' Read!

DAVID. *(reading)* 'Enter laughing! — I trust I haven't kept you waiting too long, but —'

MARLOWE. *(interrupting)* Read that again, will you?

DAVID. *(with more emphasis)* 'Enter laughing! I trust —'

MARLOWE. *(crossing to DAVID)* Mister Colman.... There is a parenthesis around 'Enter laughing' ... *(He points to the script.)* It is a stage direction.

DAVID. Oh — I'm supposed to laugh when I enter.

MARLOWE. *(drily)* Exactly! Enter laughing means you laugh when you enter! *(He takes another sip and retreats a few steps.)* Proceed.

DAVID. *(raising his hand)* May I ask a question?

MARLOWE. What is it?

DAVID. What is he laughing about?

MARLOWE. *(Sighs; walks up to DAVID.)* It is in the nature of the character. Jeff Heming is a devil-may-care young man. He breaks into a solemn family gathering for the reading of a will....

DAVID. Who died?

MARLOWE. His uncle.

DAVID. And he's laughing? Why?!

MARLOWE. *(glaring)* Because I say so!

ANGELA. You see, he's amused at the false solemnity of the others. They're only interested in the old man's money, but he...

MARLOWE. *(shouting)* The devil with it! Just let me hear

you laugh and go into the speech!

ANGELA. *(softly)* Just let him hear you laugh and go into the speech. *(She moves off.)*

DAVID. *(emitting a hollow laugh)* Hah, hah...

MARLOWE. No, no — it's an amused laugh.

DAVID. *(chuckling or gurgling foolishly)* Heh, heh, heh, heh...

MARLOWE. Amused, boy, amused.

DAVID. *(trying various laughs: weak, hearty, hysterical — and finally one ending with a question...)* Hah, hah, hah, hah??

MARLOWE. *(drily)* Splendid! Now read.

DAVID. *(reading)* I trust I haven't kept you waiting too long, but I know that in your grife ... time has no meaning.

MARLOWE. That's grief, boy ... in your *grief*, time has no meaning.

DAVID. *(imitating MARLOWE)* In your *grief* time has no meaning.

(MARLOWE sobs quietly, as he takes another sip.)

PIKE. *(reading cue)* Why are you so late, Jeff?

DAVID. *(weakly)* Heh, heh, heh...

MARLOWE. What was that?

DAVID. *(pointing to script)* It says, 'chuckles', in parenthesis.

MARLOWE. Oh? Very good. Continue.

PIKE. *(reading)* 'You can only blame yourself, Jeff.'

DAVID. *(About to read, hesitates; to MARLOWE:)* ... Should I do it the way it says? It says angry, in parenthesis.

MARLOWE. Please.

DAVID. *(to PIKE)* Will you say your part again?

PIKE. 'You can only blame yourself, Jeff.'

DAVID. *(He whirls at MARLOWE, shakes fist at him and shouts.)* That's not true, Horace and you know it!!

MARLOWE. *(Startled.... pause, then calmly:)* Would you mind waiting outside, please?

(DAVID takes fist out of MARLOWE'S face; exits, pleased with himself.)

MARLOWE. Angela, your cute one stinks!

ANGELA. You frightened him, Daddy. You frighten everyone.

MARLOWE. *(looking back)* I didn't frighten him enough. He's smiling at me.

ANGELA. He has a darling personality.

MARLOWE. Where? Where is it? .... Angela, we cannot allow him into a theatre. We are asking the audience to throw coins into a paper plate. We must have some integrity.

ANGELA. I know, but at least he looks interesting. Like a starving poet .... It's a simple part. All he has to do is say the words. Cut out everything in parenthesis.

MARLOWE. You really want him?

ANGELA. Yes! You're not going to stick me with one of the others, even if they pay more.

MARLOWE. *(resigned, to PIKE:)* Bring back the cute one. And sign up the other two.... They can move scenery or something. Ask them for eight dollars a week.

PIKE. I don't think they'll go for that much.

MARLOWE. All right, give them a scholarship. Five

dollars, four, get as much as you can.

PIKE. Maybe if you let them act...

MARLOWE. *(horrified)* Act? *(He considers this.)* Well, you can put them in the scene where they read the will.... They can be the dead man's lawyers.

(PIKE exits towards wings.)

ANGELA. Don't look so bitter, Daddy — we've had worse.

MARLOWE. Never, never!

(DAVID enters.)

MARLOWE. *(to DAVID)* Young man, I feel that you have some innate talent in you, somewhere ... and if you really apply yourself, you might make an actor, an unusual one.

DAVID. *(delighted)* You think so, sir?

MARLOWE. Well — we're going to put you on a scholar-ship here. Instead of the usual tuition, it will be five dollars a week —

DAVID. *(elated)* Five dollars! That's great; I sure could use it.

MARLOWE. Use it? What do you mean?

DAVID. I mean, I can use the extra money.

MARLOWE. No, no, dear boy. We don't pay you, you pay us.

DAVID. Oh. But I thought you said—a scholarship—

MARLOWE. Yes, I did. Ordinarily, you see, the tuition is ten dollars a week. With a scholarship, it's only five.

DAVID. *(hesitating)* Five dollars?

MARLOWE. *(impatiently)* Well, three dollars, then? If you have a burning desire to be in the theatre, surely you can manage three lousy dollars. If you have the impulse of an artist, you would steal it, if necessary.

DAVID. Yes, sir. I guess so, sir.

MARLOWE. *(Hands him script that PIKE has just given to him.)* Good.... And we feel the only to learn to act is to act. So starting this Friday night, you're to play the Jeff Heming role in my production. Here's the script; your part is marked.

DAVID. This Friday night?

MARLOWE. I want you to see the performance tonight, so you can become familiar with the role.

DAVID. Tonight?

MARLOWE. And if you have any questions, come back after the show and see me, or Mr. Pike here. Or my daughter. This is my daughter.

DAVID. She is?

MARLOWE. *(dryly)* Yes, she is.

ANGELA. I'll be glad to help you, Don. If you want me, I'll be in my dressing room.

DAVID. Tonight?

ANGELA. Yes, after the show.

DAVID. In your dressing room?

ANGELA. Yes. The play starts at eight-thirty.

DAVID. Eight-thirty. Should I eat first?

ANGELA. *(startled)* Should you..... If you want to.

MARLOWE. *(approaching them)* Work hard, young man. Work very hard.

DAVID. *(with enthusiasm)* Yes, sir! Mr. Marlowe, I want to

thank you for this opportunity and I promise to do everything I can to be really excellent.

MARLOWE. *(drily)* Fine. Goodby.

DAVID. *(to MARLOWE, PIKE, ANGELA:)* Goodbye.
Goodbye. Goodbye, Miss Marlowe.

ANGELA. Au revoir, Don.

DAVID. Yes, ma'am. *(Exits.)*

ANGELA. Well, Daddy, what do you think of him?

MARLOWE. *(looking after him, thoughtfully)* I'm not
sure ... but I think I hate that boy.

BLACKOUT

ACT ONE

Scene 4

Scene: A phone booth. Phone is on a bracket attached U.S.L. of first portal. DAVID enters and takes phone off hook.

DAVID. Hello, Operator, Jerome 8275. *(He waits.)* Hello, Papa? Listen, Papa, I won't be home for supper. No, I'm all right. I'm going to a kind of night school. For acting. Acting ... like in the movies.... No, don't put Mama on.... I'll tell you when I ... Hello, Mama.... I'll eat at a restaurant, Mama.... Eggs. Okay, meat.... No, don't wait up for me, Mama, I'll be home late.... Goodbye, Mama.... Okay, Ma, sure ... all right ... okay ... all right ... *(Hangs up. Gets coin from pocket; lifts receiver. Puts in coin.)* Operator, I got the wrong number. I wanted Tremont 8067....*(Coin drops.)* Thank you. I trust I haven't kept you waiting too long, but — *(pause)* Hello, Wanda? It's Dave. Listen to this, I went for a job in a play, and they hired me.... Yes, as an actor. There were about twelve other fellows, but they hired me.... No, I'm not kidding. Listen, I have to eat supper and get back.... I don't know, eggs or something.... Okay, meat.... So long, Wanda. *(Hangs up. Takes coin from phone; lifts receiver. Puts in coin.)* Hello, Operator, I got the wrong number.... I wanted Fordham 7648. Thanks.... *(Coin drops.)* I trust I haven't kept you waiting too long, but in my grief... *(then)* Hi, Marvin? David. I did it. No kidding, they picked me from the whole bunch. About twenty guys.... And listen, Marv ... I got a date tonight with the leading lady. Gorgeous. We're going to go over some love scenes, know what I mean? ... *(Laughs.)* You said it. *(Laughs, then seriously.)* By the way, Marv, did that laugh sound okay? Just now, when I just laughed — did that sound like a person laughing? Never mind — I'll tell you about it to-morrow. Goodbye. *(He exits.)*

End of Scene 4

ACT ONE

Scene 5

Scene: Ext. of dressing room.... DAVID and PIKE.

PIKE. You'll have to get a tuxedo for the play.

DAVID. I don't have one.

PIKE. You can get a second-hand one for about ten dollars.

DAVID. Ten dollars .... I don't....

PIKE. This is Miss Marlowe's dressing room. *(He knocks on door.)*

ANGELA. *(from off-stage)* Entrez...

PIKE. Go in.

(Int. dressing room... ANGELA in slip... David enters, stares...)

DAVID. I .... I'm sorry.... *(Starts to exit.)*

ANGELA. Come in, darling....

DAVID. *(hesitating)* But .... but you're....

ANGELA. Come in....

(DAVID turns aside from her.)

ANGELA. I'm sure this isn't the first time you've been in

a room where a girl was dressing, n'est ce pas?

DAVID. No, ma'am...

ANGELA. I thought not.

DAVID. I have a kid sister.

ANGELA. That's sweet. How did you like the play?

DAVID. Oh, I... I thought it was great. And you were great. Wow...

ANGELA. Thank you, darling. Would you hand me those stockings?

DAVID. *(staring at her legs)* Huh...?

ANGELA. Over there...

DAVID. Oh... sure. *(He hands them to her.)*

ANGELA. *(nodding toward table as she puts on stocking)* Now open two of those beers, and tell me all about yourself.

DAVID. *(staring at her as she puts on stocking)* Huh...? Oh, sure. *(He crosses to table and opens two bottles of beer, during:)* Well, I was born in the Bronx... I went to school there and I still live there and my parents want me to be a druggist, but... *(He is staring at her thigh as she smooths top of stocking; he stops speaking.)*

ANGELA. But you don't want to be a druggist.

DAVID. *(hypnotized)* Why not...? Oh, no sir, ma'am...

ANGELA. *(holding hand out)* May I? —

DAVID. Huh...? Oh... Here. *(Hands her both bottles of beer.)*

ANGELA. One of them is for you. *(Gives one back to him.)*

DAVID. *(taking it gingerly)* Oh... Uh, thank you...

ANGELA. Cheers! *(She clinks bottles and drinks.)*

(He takes a sip uneasily, and shudders.)

ANGELA. So you want to be an actor. Why do you want to be an actor? *(Puts bottle down and puts on her other stocking, adjusting it, etc.)*

DAVID. *(Staring at her; talks in short spurts.)* I ... It's exciting ... it's ... everybody watches you ... You're doing something and everybody watches you ...

ANGELA. That's a very good reason! Now, what can I do for you?

DAVID. *(tightly)* W — What do you mean?

ANGELA. About the play.

DAVID. Oh, the play... Well, that's what I wanted to tell you... I don't think I can do it.

ANGELA. Oh, why?

DAVID. There are so many words.

ANGELA. *(Steps down; sits and puts on shoes.)* Oh, no! You just have two short scenes, and the love scene with me has very little dialogue.

DAVID. I know... it's mostly kissing.

ANGELA. Yes, well — Is that so hard?

DAVID. No, that's okay... I'm a good kisser.

ANGELA. Well – then– I don't understand.

DAVID. ... Gee, Miss Marlowe ... I don't think I can do it by Friday night. So I thought I'd tell you now, so you can get someone else.

ANGELA. *(interrupting)* Don... *(She smiles at him warmly, using all her charms; dabs perfume stopper behind ears and on her cleavage.)* Don, darling... *(Sits on settee; motions him to join her.)* ... Sit here....

(He timidly sits next to her, clutching his beer bottle.)

ANGELA. Dear Don... *(Takes his hand in hers.)* Are you in love?

DAVID. You mean right now?...

ANGELA. Yes.

DAVID. *(staring in her eyes)* I think so...

ANGELA. What is Jeff trying to say in that scene? That he loves me.... Is that so hard?

DAVID. I guess not.

ANGELA. Then say it.

DAVID. What?

ANGELA. Say, "I love you."

DAVID. *(hesitantly; embarrassed)* I love you...

ANGELA. *(caressing his cheek)* ... Again ...

DAVID. *(meaning it)* I... I love you.

ANGELA. I believe you! Now if you can express that emotion more deeply, more fully...

DAVID. How? ... How????

ANGELA. *(putting arm around him)* There's only one real way to express love.... Everything else is superficial ... shallow.

DAVID. Yeah!

ANGELA. Poetry.

DAVID. What?

ANGELA. The language of love.

DAVID. You mean poems? Like Rudyard Kipling?

ANGELA. Yes! I had to say this poem in a play once, and I was in love, so I never forgot it... *(She rises, and recites, fervently.)* "If I were queen of pleasure — And you were king of pain — We'd hunt down love together — Pluck out his flying feather... — And teach his feet a measure... — And find his mouth a rein... *(She pauses.)*

DAVID. I...I...

ANGELA. If I were queen of pleasure — And you were king of pain..." You do feel it, don't you?

DAVID. *(fervently)* I do. I do.

ANGELA. *(pulling DAVID to his knees)* But that's not the only way to express love.

DAVID. Of course not.

ANGELA. I know what you're thinking ... something more turbulent, more violent, more exciting.

DAVID. Yeah, yeah....

ANGELA. "I cried for madder music and for stronger wine — But when the feast is finished and the lamps expire.. — Then falls thy shadow, Cynara... — The night is thine. *(She hugs him.)* — And I am desolate and sick of an old passion. — Yea, hungry for the lips of my desire.... *(Pushes him away. He falls to floor.)* — I have been faithful to thee, Cynara, in my fashion.."

DAVID. *(breathless)* That's wonderful.

ANGELA. I knew it. I knew that you would love poetry as I do..... *le mot juste, le mot grande....* You're a dear, dear, sensitive boy. You'll be marvelous in the play.... *(sharply)* You will do it, won't you?

DAVID. I will! I will!

ANGELA. Good.... *(She turns away, and starts adjusting her hair.)* Now, I simply must be getting home.

DAVID. Home? Now?

ANGELA. Yes, I'm frightfully tired. And you must be too, it's quite late.

DAVID. No, I'm not tired. You're sure you want me to go home? Can't we rehearse?

ANGELA. Tomorrow.

DAVID. Tomorrow?

ANGELA. *(leading him to door)* Yes, tomorrow. Till then, darling, good night.... "Good night, good night, parting is such sweet sorrow, that I will say good night till it be morrow."

(He is out; she sighs in relief, turns towards dressing table.. He bursts in.)

DAVID. "Though I've beaten you and flayed you.... — By the living God that made you.... — You're a better man than I am, Gunga Din"....

(She stares at him, stunned.... He exits.)

BLACKOUT

ACT ONE

Scene 6

Late that night. Kitchen of Kolowitz home. MOTHER, in bathrobe,
is standing at stove. FATHER, seated R. of table in pajamas,
having tea, reading newspaper.

MOTHER. *(Crosses R. above table, circles it.)* Why don't you
go to sleep, Morris? You got a day's work tomorrow.

FATHER. I'll wait.

MOTHER. *(Crosses L. below.)* I don't need your help to
wait. Go to sleep.

FATHER. I'll wait.

MOTHER. *(At L. of table.)* You'll catch a cold sitting like
that. At least put something on.

FATHER. Put on what? You're wearing my bathrobe.

MOTHER. Why? You want the bathrobe?

FATHER. No, I don't want the bathrobe. I never wear
the bathrobe.

MOTHER. *(crossing S.R.)* It's almost three o'clock. Something must have happened to him.

FATHER. Nothing happened. Go to sleep.

MOTHER. *(pause)* Why don't you ever wear the bathrobe? It's your bathrobe. I bought it for you.

FATHER. Because you always wear it.... Anyway I'm not cold.

MOTHER. Go to sleep. It's bad for your hernia! *(Crosses D.R. and D.S. of table to L.)*

FATHER. It's not bad for my hernia. When I'm sitting, my hernia is sitting.

MOTHER. *(at L. of L. chair)* You should get an operation.

FATHER. Not now. It's three o'clock in the morning.

MOTHER. *(pause)* You want more tea?

FATHER. No.

MOTHER. *(Crosses to stove.)* I'll make you more tea.

FATHER. I don't want tea.

MOTHER. Then put on your pants.

FATHER. Emma, please leave me alone. Go to sleep.

MOTHER. How can I go to sleep? Three o'clock and he's not home. What could have happened?

FATHER. Please, Emma, you're making me crazy, and you're making yourself crazy. Go to sleep.

MOTHER. *(Rising, crosses L.)* Call up somebody.

FATHER. *(rising, putting paper on table)* Who? You want me to call the police?

MOTHER. *(crossing to L. of table)* No, I don't want to get mixed up with the police. Call up Harry.

FATHER. *(rising)* Harry? Why should I call up Harry?

MOTHER. He's your brother, why shouldn't you call him up?

FATHER. But why should I call him up, in the middle of the night? What could he do?

MOTHER. Harry is a business man. He has a good lawyer. He'll know what to do.

FATHER. Emma, make me some tea. *(Sits.)*

MOTHER. *(She crosses to stove.)* You didn't want tea.

FATHER. Now I want.

MOTHER. Why won't you call up Harry?

FATHER. Emma, please. At three o'clock, I don't call my brother for advice about my son.

MOTHER. *(Crosses R. to behind him, her hands on his shoulders.)* I'm worried, Morris. I don't know what to think. what should we do?

FATHER. *(gently)* All right, Emma. It's all right. You'll see. He's all right.

DAVID. *(Enters, falsely casual.)* Hi. *(Crosses to U.S. of table.)* What are you doing up so late?

MOTHER. You hear him, Morris? *(Rises, crosses L. below table.)* What are we doing up so late, he asks. What are *we* doing up so late? *(with heavy sarcasm)* It was too hot to sleep, so we got up to play a game of dominos. *(Sits, L.)*

FATHER. *(rising to S.R. of DAVID)* Mama was worried about you, David.

MOTHER. *(Rises. D.L. few steps, then to U.L. of table.)* I was worried? And you weren't? Papa was so worried he wanted to call Uncle Harry. Where were you?

DAVID. There was nothing to worry about. I was okay.

MOTHER. Why didn't you call us to let us know *what*?

DAVID. I did call, Ma. I spoke to you and told you that I'd be late.

MOTHER. *(Crosses D.R. below table.)* You called *yesterday* and said you'd be home late. Three o'clock isn't late. Three o'clock is tomorrow!

DAVID. *(Crosses to D.L. of table.)* I went to night school,

Ma. I told you and Pa about it.

MOTHER. *(crossing U.R.)* What kind of night school stays open till four in the morning? A night school for tramps?

FATHER. *(crossing U.S. to her.)* Emma, please. You'll wake up the whole neighborhood.

DAVID. *(L. of S.L. chair)* I called you, Ma. I told you I was taking a course in acting.

MOTHER. *(crossing to above the table)* You told me, you told me! Never mind what you told me. Let me tell you something. Where were you?

FATHER. *(crossing to S.R. of R. chair)* David, a night school I can understand. Nine, ten o'clock, I can understand. But three o'clock is no night school.

MOTHER. A night school for tramps!

DAVID. It's a school for actors.

MOTHER. Bums and tramps!

DAVID. I had to stay later, Ma. To study my part. Like homework.

MOTHER. *(to FATHER)* What kind of homework? *(to DAVID)* The first day you don't get homework. The first day you meet the teacher, you get your books, you don't get homework till four, five o'clock in the morning. Where were you?

DAVID. It's an acting school, Ma. It's not like high school. Don't you believe me?

MOTHER. *(Picks up cup and saucer.)* All right, I believe you, I believe you. If you don't want to tell us, I believe you. *(Puts cup and saucer on stove.)* Go to sleep. Soon it's time to get up.

DAVID. Okay. Good night, Ma. Good night, Pa. *(Starts to exit.)*

MOTHER. And no more acting school.

DAVID. *(Turns back. Crosses to S.L. of MOTHER.)* What!? Why not? I have a rehearsal tomorrow night. I have to be there.

MOTHER. I said no more acting school. Tell him, Morris.

FATHER. David, you heard what Mama said.

MOTHER. That's how you tell him?

FATHER. *(crossing below table to L. of table)* David, what do you need acting for? You're worrying Mama for nothing.

DAVID. But, Ma, the man in charge says I'm very good. He picked me out of about forty guys.

MOTHER. David, you have a job. Do a good job. You're going to be a druggist. You'll be a good druggist. You'll get married. Be a good husband, a good father. A good tramp till four o'clock in the morning, you don't have to be.

DAVID. But listen, Ma —

MOTHER. Tell him, Morris.

FATHER. David — god night. *(Crosses, sits L. of table.)*

(MOTHER crosses D.R. few steps, arms folded, facing away from him.)

DAVID. *(Extends hand to FATHER.)* Okay. Goodnight, Pa.

FATHER. *(shaking hands)* Good night, David.

DAVID. *(Crosses playfully to S.L. of MOTHER.)* Good night, Ma. *(He puts his arms around her and kisses her cheek.)*

MOTHER. You hungry?

DAVID. No, I'm okay.

MOTHER. What kind of junk did you eat?

DAVID. *(Poses like ape-man.)* I ate okay, Ma. Meat. Good night, Ma. *(Exits S.R. of C. wall.)*

FATHER. He's a good boy, Emma.

MOTHER. *(Crosses to above table.)* Did I say he wasn't a good boy? I know he's a good boy. But he's still a boy. He has to be told.

FATHER. I know.

MOTHER. If we could afford to send him to pharmacy college—

FATHER. I know. I know.

MOTHER. *(Puts cups on stove.)* Go to sleep. And in the morning, you talk to him. Acting! A madness suddenly got into him. *(Picks up newspaper from table.)*

FATHER. *(rising to U.S. of L. chair; gently, to himself)* I once saw Jacob Adler on Second Avenue in a play by William Shakespeare. Gold! Pure gold!

MOTHER. *I'll* talk to him! *(Exits U.R. of C. wall.)*

BLACKOUT

ACT ONE

Scene 7

Scene: The shop. In the morning.

At Rise: MARVIN and DAVID enter from upstage of S.L. second portal. DAVID turns on buffer. He crosses R. and hangs his jacket. MARVIN crosses to S.L. of buffing machine. DAVID buffs a piece of metal and turns off machine, picks up file and works on piece of metal.

MARVIN. You were with that actress half the night? *(DAVID nods.)* Is that why you came to work an hour late this morning? *(DAVID nods.)* You were in her dressing room? *(DAVID nods.)* How come you went into her dressing room? Did she ask you?

DAVID. Not exactly.

MARVIN. What then?

DAVID. She wanted to rehearse, so I said — *(elegantly)* "Wouldn't it perhaps be cozier if we rehearsed in your dressing room, where we wouldn't be disturbed?"

MARVIN. Just like that?

DAVID. Uh-huh.

MARVIN. You talked in that phony way?

DAVID. That's how they talk — you should have heard her.

MARVIN. What do you mean?

DAVID. She talked to me in poetry!

MARVIN. *(awed)* Wow! Did you understand her?

DAVID. The things she was doing, she could of talked Turkish, I would have understood!

MARVIN. *(sitting, L. of table)* No kidding!

DAVID. Marve, won't they miss you upstairs?

MARVIN. Nah. So what happened after you got into her dressing room?

DAVID. Well, we talked a little bit — and then we started to, you know, get comfortable.

MARVIN. You mean, undress?

DAVID. Sort of.

MARVIN. What do you mean? Who took off what? I mean, did you help her take anything off? Or did she help you?

DAVID. *(sarcastically)* No, we called a kid in from the street — *(pause)* and gave him a quarter — *(pause)* and he undressed us! *(Pulls script out of pocket, crosses D.R., tosses metal and file into tray on table.)* Listen, Marve, I've got to study my script!

MARVIN. *(Crosses R. to DAVID.)* Just tell me what happened after that. I mean, after you got comfortable. *(U.R.S. of table)* I mean, who started it? I mean, who kissed who first?

DAVID. I'll tell you the rest some other time, Marve. And you better get back upstairs, before you get fired.

MARVIN. *(Crosses D.S.L.)* Look, just tell me one thing — just one thing — yes or no? — Did you or didn't you?

DAVID. *(hedging)* Well — not exactly.

MARVIN. What do you mean, not exactly? With a thing

like that, it's either you did or you didn't! *(Crosses U.C., then sits S.L. of table.)*

DAVID. Well, I'm seeing her again tonight, so it's a cinch. *(Crosses U.C. and sits on stool.)* Listen, can you lend me some money, Marve?

MARVIN. Gee, I don't know, Dave. How much?

DAVID. About ten dollars.

MARVIN. Ten dollars?

DAVID. I have to get a tuxedo for the play.

MARVIN. You know I haven't got that kind of money.

DAVID. I'll have to get it from Foreman. I'll have to make up some kind of story.

MARVIN. Listen, Dave —

DAVID. What?

MARVIN. What are you going to do about Wanda? I mean now that you have this actress —

DAVID. I know. I'm going to have lunch with her today. Maybe I'll just tell her.

MARVIN. You'll tell her? Gee, she'll feel rotten.

DAVID. I don't know. Maybe I won't tell her. *(rising, crossing to S.L.)* My God, I can't tear myself into a million pieces.

MARVIN. I wish I had your troubles.

DAVID. *(Remembers.)* Oh my God!

MARVIN. What's the matter?

DAVID. I have a lunch date with Miss B. today. I forgot all about it.

MARVIN. The zoftig bookkeeper?

DAVID. *(Crosses below table to phone.)* She practically begged me for a date. Now I have to call it off.

MARVIN. Boy, I sure wish I had your troubles.

DAVID. Operator, Longacre 2121.

MARVIN. Dave, are there any other actresses around? I mean in the play? I thought maybe you could introduce me. Nah, I wouldn't know who does what first.

DAVID. *(into phone)* Hello, Miss B? Laura? ... This is Dave, Dave Kolowitz, from Foreman Machines.... Yes, your lunch date. Only I have to call off our date.... You see, I was put in that play I told you about and they called a rehearsal this afternoon.... It starts tomorrow night, I think. I would invite you as my guest at the play.... What? You're going to a banquet of what? Oh, I didn't know your friend was a hat salesman. *(Abruptly, as FOREMAN enters.)* No, there's no one here by that name. *(Hangs up, picks up piece of metal and file; works.)*

FOREMAN. *(Takes off hat and coat, and hangs them up on hook S.L. of C. shelves. Gets apron from hook.)* You're here again. Maybe I should make you a partner!

MARVIN. *(Starts to rise.)* I was just leaving.

FOREMAN. *(putting MARVIN back into chair; too friendly)* No hurry. Sit down; have a glass tea.

MARVIN. No.

FOREMAN. *(at U.S. of table)* Maybe a game pinochle.

MARVIN. *(rising, crossing U.L. to door)* I just came in to say hello.

FOREMAN. And if you don't come in to say hello, I wouldn't be able to eat my supper?

(MARVIN exits.)

FOREMAN. What kind of a job does he have, that they pay him and he's always here? *(putting on apron)* Any calls?

DAVID. No.

(Phone rings.)

FOREMAN. *(into phone)* Hello? ... Who? Mona Lisa Hats? ... So what do you want, Kaplan? Maybe you need a new shuttle.... Why didn't you call earlier? ... You did? What time did you call? I was out but my boy was here.... He wasn't here? Where was he? ... All right, I'll come look at it later. Kaplan, don't be an old woman; I said I'll come. I'll come when I'll come. Maybe a little earlier! *(Hangs up phone, moves machine from U.S. bench to table.)* So — good afternoon! *(Sits C. above table.)*

DAVID. *(Crosses L. to U.S. of FOREMAN.)* I'm sorry I was a little late, Mr. Foreman. It was only about fifteen minutes.

FOREMAN. Fifteen minutes or fifteen hours, on time is on time —

DAVID. You're right, Mr. Foreman. *(Pats FOREMAN'S shoulder.)*

FOREMAN. *(rising, crossing S.R. a few steps)* If you're supposed to open and you're not here and Mona Lisa calls with a big order, an emergency. Nobody answers by us, they call somebody else.

(DAVID gets broom and sweeps floor, S.L.)

FOREMAN. What are you sweeping first thing in the morning? We're not going to make dirt today?

DAVID. I'm sorry, I was thinking of something else. *(Hangs broom U.S.L.)*

(FOREMAN turns on buffing machine, buffs piece of metal.)

DAVID. *(Yells.)* Mr. Foreman.

FOREMAN. Yes.

DAVID. Could I borrow ten dollars till pay day?

FOREMAN. I didn't hear.

DAVID. *(Yells.)* Could I borrow ten dollars till pay day?

(Machine cuts off in middle of DAVID'S speech. FOREMAN stares at DAVID for a moment, turns on the buffer again. Then turns it off, tosses metal on bench, takes machine from bench to table.)

FOREMAN. *(sitting at table)* What does a boy like you need ten dollars for? Food you got, clothes you got, carfare you got. What do you need ten dollars for? For tootsie rolls? *(There is a pause. He rises, goes to DAVID.)* David, are you in some trouble?

DAVID. Of course not, Mr. Foreman.

FOREMAN. Tell your father, David. If you're in trouble, always tell your father.

DAVID. It's no trouble, Mr. Foreman. The reason I didn't tell my father — it's for a birthday present for him.

FOREMAN. For your father?

DAVID. Yes. I want to buy him something—

(FOREMAN stares at him.)

DAVID. A — a new prayer shawl.

FOREMAN. *(Looks at him for a moment, then smiles.)* A prayer shawl? You're a good boy, David. For that you got a right to lend. You're a good boy.

DAVID. *(very relieved)* Thanks, Mr. Foreman.

FOREMAN. *(Takes machine from table to U.S. bench.)* And I can save you money, too — I'll get it for you wholesale.

DAVID. *(Moves chair R. of table to R. of U.S. bench.)* Well, no, Mr. Foreman, I have one picked out that—

FOREMAN. Please, David, about prayer shawls I know a little more than you.

DAVID. You don't have to bother, Mr. Foreman, after all, it's my present to my father—

FOREMAN. It's still your present, but I'll help out a little — I'll get it when I go out for lunch. *(Puts machine on D.S. bench, sits.)*

DAVID. Oh, Mr. Foreman.

FOREMAN. *(working on machine at bench)* What?

DAVID. *(Sits chair, R. of bench.)* I'm going to have to eat my lunch out today. I forgot to bring my lunch.

FOREMAN. *(still working)* You forgot? Your mother made you lunch and you forgot to take it?

DAVID. Well, I didn't exactly forget — my father took my lunch by mistake.

FOREMAN. He took your lunch?

DAVID. By mistake.

FOREMAN. Then, why didn't you take his?

DAVID. He didn't have one — my father doesn't eat lunch!

FOREMAN. *(Moves stool U.S. Leans elbow on U.S. bench as he faces DAVID.)* He doesn't eat lunch?

DAVID. I mean, he goes out for lunch.

FOREMAN. Then, why did he take your lunch?

DAVID. It was a strange mistake. He thought — they were dress samples. He brought some samples home to work on, and he took my lunch instead of the samples. I guess he's nervous on account of his birthday!

FOREMAN. He's nervous about his birthday? Your father?

(DAVID doesn't answer.)

FOREMAN. *(Turns back to his work.)* All right, I'll bring you a corned beef sandwich when I come back.

DAVID. No, I — since my father took my lunch, I made an appointment for lunch.

FOREMAN. *(rising to S.L. of stool; shacked)* An appointment! A nothing, a peanut has an appointment! *(Shakes his head, disbelievingly.)* America!

(DAVID gets jacket from hook on S.R. wall and exits.)

BLACKOUT

ACT ONE

Scene 8

Scene: Section of dairy restaurant on platform, pushed on from D.L.
WANDA, seated S.L. at table by herself, looking at menu.
She is an attractive, 17-year-old. WAITER stands U.S.
of table.

WAITER. You ready to order?
WANDA. Not yet. I have an appointment. *(Looks at menu again.)*

(WAITER exits upstage of S.L. second portal. DAVID enters from U.R. and heads towards WANDA.)

DAVID. Hello, Wanda. You waiting long?
WANDA. No, just a few minutes.

(DAVID sits, R. of table.)

WANDA. David, I can't tell you how I feel about your getting a part in a real play. You must be so nervous about tomorrow night — I know I am.
DAVID. I don't know if there's going to be any tomorrow night.

52

WANDA. Why? What happened? They changed their mind?

DAVID. Well, it's just that I have to have a costume for the play tomorrow night. A full dress suit. And I haven't got the money.

WANDA. How much is it?

DAVID. About ten dollars, I guess. I asked everybody.

WANDA. David, I have ten dollars. I'm supposed to buy a dress, but I can get it another time.

DAVID. Gee, Wanda, I can't take money from you.

WANDA. You're not taking it. It's a loan. *(Digs into purse which has been on her lap.)*

DAVID. I know, but even so—

WANDA. Please, David — I want to. When I see you on the stage, I'll know it's my suit. Here. Really. I want to. *(Puts it on table.)*

DAVID. *(He looks at it out of the corner of his eye as he picks it up, and counts it, then puts it in his pocket. Takes her hands in his.)* Gee, you're a great girl, Wanda. No kidding. I'll pay you back right after payday.

WANDA. There's no hurry. Really.

DAVID. Well, then I'll pay you half this payday, and half next.

WANDA. Whenever you want to.

DAVID. I tell you what. I'll pay you three dollars a week. And one dollar the fourth week.

WANDA. I'm really happy I can help. Honest. Do you know your part yet? Is it a very big part?

DAVID. Well, I've been studying it, on the subway and at home. I hardly slept last night, trying to memorize it.

WANDA. Is it a lot?

DAVID. I'm just in two scenes, but it's an important part. Kind of a playboy. I have to rehearse tonight.

WANDA. Do you think I can come and watch?

DAVID. Yeah. I guess so. If you want to.

WANDA. You'll be wonderful. I just know it. A playboy!

WAITER. *(Enters from S.L. above second portal. At U.S. of table.)* You ready to order yet?

WANDA. *(picking up menu and looking at it)* Gosh, I haven't even looked at the menu. I'll tell you, I'll just have coke. *(Gives menu to WAITER.)*

DAVID. Me, too. Coke.

WAITER. Two cokes for the table?

DAVID. That's all.

(WAITER takes tablecloth and menu off with him as he exits L. behind second portal.)

WANDA. What kind of playboy are you in the play, David? Do you make love or — anything like that?

DAVID. *(laughing)* Well, yes, in one scene, I make love to the leading lady.

WANDA. *(laughing)* Oh? You do?

(They stop laughing simultaneously.)

WANDA. Is she nice looking?

DAVID. She's okay.

WANDA. *(pause)* Very nice-looking?

DAVID. Oh, I'd say so.

WANDA. She must be pretty old — I mean, to be a leading lady.

DAVID. *(slight pause)* No, she's not so old.

WANDA. David? Is there something you want to tell me?

DAVID. No. I don't think so. Not really. I guess not.

WANDA. David, you know we always said that we should be honest with each other.

DAVID. I know that.

WANDA. Is there someone else, David?

DAVID. *(hurriedly)* No, no. Nothing like that!

WANDA. Well, what is it, then?

DAVID. *(quickly)* It's *something* like that —

(She is still looking at him.)

DAVID. — but not exactly.

WANDA. Is it the actress?

DAVID. Well, in a way.

WANDA. Do you like her?

DAVID. Well, I don't hate her.

WANDA. And how does she feel about you?

DAVID. Well, she doesn't hate me, either.

WANDA. Then it's mutual.

DAVID. What can I do? That's life. You want me to be honest, don't you?

WANDA. Absolutely. Of course.

DAVID. *(long pause)* And then there's also this book-keeper—

WANDA. Another one?

DAVID. No, of course not. What do you think I am, a sex maniac?

WANDA. *(after pause)* Have you had an affair with her?
DAVID. Which one?

(WANDA is shocked.)

DAVID. No, no, neither. Not yet. I mean, no. *(pause)* Do you want your ten dollars back?
WANDA. No. Of course not. I better be going.
DAVID. Gee, Wanda, I hope you're not sore or anything.
WANDA. *(rising; burning, but covering it)* Of course not. What's there to be sore about?
DAVID. *(sincerely explaining)* Wanda, I want you to know that even though I may be attracted to other girls, you're still the only girl in the world I want to tell about those other girls to.
WANDA. *(outraged)* Thank you. *(Exits, L.)*

(Platform is pulled off L. as lights dim out.)

ACT ONE

Scene 9

Scene: The shop. Empty at rise. DAVID enters from S.L. upstage of second portal, carrying package. He is very excited. He crosses to D.S. table, puts machine and tray on U.S. bench, puts box on table. He takes off his jacket which he hangs up U.L.S. He turns to box, opens it, takes out jacket, admires it, puts it on, crosses from S.R., D.S. to mirror on U.R. wall. He jumps several times, trying to see himself. He goes to table, takes out flat top hat, is surprised when it opens, puts it on. He does a mock sword fight from S.R. to S.L., then crosses U.S. and gets grease from jar on shelf, U.C. He puts finger in grease and paints moustache on. He pantomimes being a villain. He gets oil can from U.S. bench and turns it upside down and pretends to drink as FOREMAN enters with box. DAVID puts oil can back and crosses to D.R. corner of shop.

FOREMAN. What can I do for you, mister? *(Puts box on L.S. chair, hangs up coat and hat on hook S.L. of shelves on C. wall, and turns to DAVID.)* David? What?

DAVID. *(Crosses D.S., syops D.L. of D.S. bench.)* Nothing, Mr. Foreman. I guess I'd better oil this machine. *(Crosses up, picks up machine and oil can, starts to oil machine. He paces above table to S.R., then S.L.)*

FOREMAN. *(Follows him below table to S.L., then to S.R. He leans on S.R. end of U.S. bench.)* "Nothing, Mr. Foreman!" A boy puts on a tuxedo with a fake moustache — what's the matter? "Nothing, Mr. Foreman!" All right, so it's nothing.

(There is a pause. DAVID, at S.L., uncomfortable, doesn't answer.)

FOREMAN. Explain me, David. I'm not a hundred-percent American, so maybe I don't understand so good. Maybe it's natural in America a boy should put on a fake moustache with grease in the middle of work! Maybe it's a special Yankee holiday!

DAVID. *(simply explaining)* I was just practicing, Mr. Foreman — I'm going to be an actor. *(Takes off hat and coat. Puts them back in box. Takes off the moustache with cold cream and rag which are on U.S. bench.)*

FOREMAN. *(pause)* An actor?

(DAVID nods.)

FOREMAN. An actor on a stage?

(DAVID nods.)

FOREMAN. *(Sits on S.R. chair.)* Oh boy, oh boy! *(rising, to S.R. of stool; severely)* Listen, David, what you do at night is your own business. But here you have to act like a person, with no foolishness with the tuxedo and the moustache in the shop. Here I don't need no Greta Garbo.

DAVID. *(U.L. of table)* I know, Mr. Foreman.

FOREMAN. *(There is a pause. He moves machine from U.S. bench to D.S. table.)* I brought the prayer shawl for your father.

DAVID. *(bewildered)* What?

FOREMAN. *(Sits C. Puts tuxedo box on top of prayer shawl on S.L. chair.)* The prayer shawl! For your father's birthday.

DAVID. Oh, Oh! Thanks, Mr. Foreman.

FOREMAN. *(working on machine)* $2.50. A four dollar prayer shawl. I'll take it off this week's pay.

DAVID. *(Waves cloth in air.)* Okay. Sure.

FOREMAN. *(to himself)* An actor! An actor I've got for a helper!

(DAVID crosses D.L.S.)

FOREMAN. Listen David, is it all right for a fancy actor to make a delivery to Traymore Hats?

DAVID. Sure, Mr. Foreman.

FOREMAN. So, please, do me a favor and put on your tuxedo and fake moustache and deliver this machine.

(DAVID starts putting his jacket on.)

FOREMAN. And get a receipt.

DAVID. Oh, one thing, Mr. Foreman.... I have to leave a little early tonight — maybe an hour early — I'll make it up next week.

FOREMAN. *(Stares at him.)* An hour early? Why? What?

DAVID. Well, it's my father's birthday and—

FOREMAN. *(Rises and crosses R. a few steps.)* Again your

father's birthday! Who is your father, George Washington? Maybe we should close up shop for his birthday!

DAVID. Well, the thing is, Mr. Foreman — tomorrow's the play, so I have to rehearse today. It's very important.

FOREMAN. So what's with your father's birthday?

DAVID. *(lamely)* Well — I want to surprise him by being in the play, on his birthday—

FOREMAN. *(Bewildered, gives up.)* All right, all right. I'm all mixed up with the play and the birthday and the acting. All right. So deliver the machine, and don't bother coming back today.

(DAVID picks up machine and package with suit.)

FOREMAN. And get a receipt and bring the receipt tomorrow. On time!

DAVID. Okay. Thanks, Mr. Foreman. *(Starts to exit.)*

FOREMAN. Where you going? You forgot your father's present.

(DAVID crosses back, gets shawl box from chair, then exits.)

FOREMAN. *(Calls after him.)* On time. If you want to keep the job; no more half day's work. You hear, Mr. Actor?

FADE

ACT ONE

Scene 10

Set: The stage ..... MARLOWE and ANGELA.....

MARLOWE. Well, where is your new boy? That James Monroe?

ANGELA. His name is Don Colman, and he'll be here soon, Daddy.

MARLOWE. If he's not here in two minutes, we'll use one of the phony lawyers.

(DAVID enters, carrying boxes.)

ANGELA. There he is. Come here quickly, Don.

DAVID. *(puffing)* I'm sorry I'm late, Mister Marlowe ... the train ... the train ...

MARLOWE. I know, the train, the train ... Nevermind! Do you know your lines?

ANGELA. Of course he does. *(to DAVID)* Of course you do! *(to MARLOWE)* He's a very bright boy. *(to DAVID)* Aren't you, darling?

DAVID. Well, I studied it a lot... *(Walks to MARLOWE.)*

(ANGELA stands nearby.)

61

MARLOWE. We'll try your second scene first.

DAVID. The second scene?

ANGELA. The one you do with me, dear.... *(Illustrates, hug and kiss.)*

DAVID. Oh, the love one... *(to MARLOWE)* You want me to recite it?

MARLOWE. *(bewildered)* Recite it?

DAVID. *(Closes eyes.)* I say, "Well, here you are, my dear," and she says, "As you can see," and I say, "It's good to find one human being in this.....

MARLOWE. No, no, don't recite it! Let's try to act it, shall we? .... Acting, my boy, is style. The main thing about acting is to have a flair, to enjoy the stage. I enjoy the stage and that reaches them out there. They'll remember me, some of them. They may not know who I am but they go away thinking, "That old bastard has style!" .... Do you understand what I'm saying?

DAVID. I think so, sir.

MARLOWE. Good.... Now let's begin the scene.... Harriet is sitting on the couch....

DAVID. Who's Harriet?

ANGELA. Me. That's my name in the play....

MARLOWE. Now, you enter from upstage. On cue. Do you know your cue?

DAVID. My what....?

MARLOWE. *(shouting)* Your cue!

ANGELA. Don, when I take out a cigarette, that's your cue. Like this. *(She does it.)*

DAVID. Oh, sure, I know that.

MARLOWE. You enter and offer her a light. Now, let's do it.

DAVID. Yes sir. *(He exits off to the wings.)*

(ANGELA, seated on couch, takes cigarette from bag. David enters, carrying boxes.)

MARLOWE. Put those damn boxes down!
DAVID. Yes sir. *(Puts them on couch.)*
MARLOWE. Not on the set! Pike get rid of them.

(PIKE takes boxes.)

DAVID. It's my tuxedo.
ANGELA. Trust Pike. He'll take good care of it. Now, try your entrance, Don.
MARLOWE. *(as DAVID exits)* Remember, you're a dashing, elegant young man. Shall we try it?

(ANGELA, seated, takes cigarette out of purse ... looks for match.... DAVID leaps into room.)

MARLOWE. No, no.... Don't leap in. You're a gentleman, not a kangaroo.... Take it easy, dammit.... Walk, saunter, be debonaire.... *(He illustrates walk.)*

(DAVID imitates him, very stiffly.)

MARLOWE. My boy, the idea is to have rhythm. Count, if you have to.... You can count?
DAVID. Oh. yes sir.
MARLOWE. *(sarcastically)* How high?
DAVID. Pretty darn high.

*(MARLOWE walks downstage in rhythm; DAVID tries to keep
in step.)*

MARLOWE. Not with me, by yourself.

*(DAVID walks to ANGELA, with "fancy" step, stops and looks
at MARLOWE.)*

MARLOWE. *(drily)* Fine....

*(DAVID tries to light match, unsuccessfully, as ANGELA holds
cigarette.)*

DAVID. *(embarrassed)* I'm not used to.... I don't .... I....
*(The match lights unexpectedly, burning him; he drops lit
match.)* Ouch!

(MARLOWE groans.)

ANGELA. Daddy, why don't I light my own cigarette?
It'll speed everything up and it's perfectly natural. I
always thought it was so false to have my cigarette hanging
out.

MARLOWE. *(exasperated)* All right, all right! *(to DAVID)*
She'll light her own cigarette. Do you understand?

DAVID. Yes, sir.

MARLOWE. Splendid! *(very politely)* Now, let me hear
the words.

DAVID. Shall I go back?

MARLOWE. *(sarcastically)* Si'l vous plait!

(ANGELA lights cigarette. DAVID reenters, goes to love seat.)

MARLOWE. Fine! Now talk!

(DAVID hesitates.)

MARLOWE. Recite!

DAVID. *(to ANGELA; reciting without emotion)* 'Well, here you are, my dear.' *(His lips move with her line, as:)*

ANGELA. 'As you can see.'

DAVID. *(turning to her; arm swinging)* 'It's good to find one human being in this ridiculous place.' *(arm stops) (His lips move with ANGELA'S, as:)*

ANGELA. 'Is that how you feel about the others?'

DAVID. 'Let's not talk about the others. It's you I'm interested in.'

ANGELA. 'Oh! When you say "interested," how do you mean interested?'

(DAVID'S lips move.)

MARLOWE. Young man, let the lady have her lines. Keep your mouth shut when she's speaking. She talks ... you answer. You talk ... she answers. It's what they call conversation. You understand?

DAVID. Yes, sir.

(MARLOWE takes bottle from pocket; sips through straw.)

ANGELA. Daddy, should you be drinking?

MARLOWE. Yes! Start again.

DAVID. *(reading quickly and without emotion)* 'Well, here you are, my dear.' *(Keeps his lips tightly closed on her lines, below:)*

ANGELA. 'As you can see.'

DAVID. 'It's good to find one human being in this ridiculous place.'

ANGELA. 'Is that how you feel about the others?'

DAVID. 'Let's not talk about the others. It's you I'm interested in.'

MARLOWE. *Oh God!*

ANGELA. 'Really? When you say "interested", *how* do you mean interested?'

DAVID. 'In the only way a man can be interested in a woman. I love you, Harriet.'

ANGELA. Do you, Jeff? Do you really?

DAVID. 'You know I do...' *(to MARLOWE; timidly)* Do I kiss your daughter now or just during the show?

MARLOWE. Now, please. Exactly as in the show.

DAVID. *(hesitantly)* But... I'm standing and she's sitting.

MARLOWE. *(drily)* That does present a problem, doesn't it? What would you suggest?

DAVID. Should I lean over?

MARLOWE. *(Rises.)* Sit down, man. Sit down! When you say, 'I love you, Harriet,' ... *(tearfully)* ... sit, for God's sake, down! *(Sits.)*

ANGELA. Daddy, please.... It's his first time.

MARLOWE. Go ahead...

ANGELA. 'Is that how you feel about the others?'

DAVID. What others?

ANGELA. In the play, dear.

DAVID. Oh.

ANGELA. 'Is that how you feel about the others?'

DAVID. 'Let's not talk about the others. It's you I'm interested in. I love you, Harriet!'

ANGELA. 'Do you really, Jeff?'

DAVID. *(He sits.)* You know I do. *(long kiss)*

(ANGELA pulls away — DAVID pulls her back; continuous kiss.)

MARLOWE. Your line — your next line.

DAVID. Oh.... *(mumbles to self, recapping quickly)* Do you, Jeff? You know I do. Kiss. Please forgive me, I didn't mean that. *(then, to ANGELA)* 'Please forgive me, I didn't mean that.'

ANGELA. 'Are you sure you didn't mean it?'

DAVID. *(rattles, flatly)* 'Yes, my dear, I'm afraid I did. But you mustn't trust me, Harriet. I don't trust myself, really.'

MARLOWE. *(suddenly shouts)* Dammit, can't you talk like a human being? Can't you behave like a human being? You are human, aren't you? ... Or, aren't you — ?

DAVID. *(Rises; slowly; quietly; hurt.)* Mister Marlowe, if you think I'm not good, then just tell me. And if you want me to go, I'll go. But I don't think you should yell at me like that.

MARLOWE. Well, I'm encouraged. You're beginning to sound human.

DAVID. If you want me to do it again... ?

MARLOWE. *(rises)* No, I've had enough for today. I'm sick. I'm nauseous!

DAVID. Mister Marlowe, I know I wasn't very good...

MARLOWE. *You* know it, *I* know it. *(drily)* Now our job is to keep that little secret from the audience.

BLACKOUT

ACT TWO

Scene 1

Scene: The stage .... ANGELA and DAVID .... immediately following previous scene.

DAVID. Gee, Miss Marlowe, your father is right. I can't do it.

ANGELA. Don darling, you can do it. And please call me Angela.

DAVID. *(shaking his head)* Boy, was I rotten.

ANGELA. Don. It was your first time. You were trying ... and some things you did quite well.

DAVID. Like what?

ANGELA. *(thinking)* Well .... the kiss .... you did the kiss very well.... It was quite convincing.

DAVID. Well .... you did most of it.

ANGELA. Dear Don ... when I do a romantic scene, I have to feel something ... a je ne sais quoi .... about that person.

DAVID. Do I make you feel that thing?

ANGELA. You really do....

(WANDA enters, unnoticed by them.)

ANGELA. And by tomorrow night, you and I will work beautifully together. *(She kisses him.)* You must trust me. *(Kisses him again.)*

DAVID. I do...

ANGELA. *(over his shoulder, to WANDA)* Is there something you want?

DAVID. *(softly)* In what way...?

ANGELA. Are you looking for someone?

DAVID. *(turns)* Oh, hello there!

WANDA. I'm sorry to interrupt.

DAVID. Oh no... We were just —

WANDA. Yes, I know.

ANGELA. We were just rehearsing, my dear.

DAVID. Wanda, this is Miss Marlowe, the actress. *(to ANGELA)* Are we finished rehearsing?

ANGELA. Yes. It's quite late. And Don darling, every word I said to you was true. ....You two run along now ... Gather ye rosebuds while ye may...Old time is still a flying....Au revoir, Don darling.... *(She exits.)*

WANDA. *(looking after her)* What did she mean by that?

DAVID. By what?

WANDA. 'Don darling'...

DAVID. Oh, that's my stage-name.

WANDA. Don Darling...?

DAVID. No.. Don Colman is my stage-name. Darling is what she calls me.

WANDA. She does...?

DAVID. Well, she's an actress.

WANDA. *(coldly)* David, or Don, I'm sorry I disturbed you. I'm going home. *(She starts off.)*

DAVID. Wait a second, Wanda, I'll take you home.

WANDA. Never mind. I'd rather go home alone.

DAVID. Don't be silly, I can't let you go home alone, especially looking like that.

WANDA. What's wrong with how I look?

DAVID. Nothing, absolutely nothing. You look very appetizing, in fact. *(Touches her arm.)*

WANDA. *(pulling her arm away)* Thank you.

DAVID. How come you wore that dress?

WANDA. *(embarrassed, looking away from him)* Well — it's the sexiest one I have — and since you seem to be interested in girls for physical reasons—

DAVID. Gee, Wanda, just because I'm attracted to other girls doesn't mean I stopped being attracted to you.

WANDA. Really?

DAVID. Of course, really.

WANDA. You want me to help you with your part?

DAVID. What?

WANDA. You said you were worried about remembering your lines.

DAVID. All right, if you want to.

(They cross U.S. to chaise and sit. She is seated S.R. of him. He takes script from pocket.)

DAVID. This is the part I'm most worried about. Just read the lines that say "Harriet" — *(Up.)* "Well, here you are, my dear."

WANDA. *(Reads.)* "As you can see."

DAVID. *(stamping his foot)* "It's good to find one human being in this ridiculous place."

WANDA. "Is that how you feel about the others?"

DAVID. *(Stamps foot.)* "Let's not talk about the others. It's you I'm interested in."

WANDA. *(She looks at his foot, then speaks.)* "Really? In what way?"

DAVID. *(Stamps foot.)* "In the only way a man can be interested in a woman. I love you, Harriet."

WANDA. *(Looks at his foot again.)* "Do you really — Jeff?"

DAVID. "You know I do!"

WANDA. *(Looks up from script, gently.)* That's all there is here.

DAVID. *(Points at parenthesis.)* No, it isn't — there's something in parenthesis.

(He kisses her. They leap up, embarrassed, at PIKE'S entrance.)

PIKE. *(entering from S.L. above second portal)* All right, clear the stage. Everybody out. *(Puts D.R. chair U.S. of curtain line, moves coffe table to U.R.)*

(They rise. DAVID puts script in hip pocket, gets boxes. They step D.C.S. off platform. PIKE closes curtain, exits U.S.)

DAVID. *(at S.L. of her)* Do you have to go right home?

WANDA. *(hesitates)* It's pretty late.

DAVID. Would your mother be angry if you stayed out a little longer?

WANDA. No, I don't think so. But you have a very important day ahead of you, David.

DAVID. *(gently)* Tonight's important, too.

WANDA. Is it?

DAVID. I think so. Yes.

WANDA. *(looking front)* Where do you want to go?

DAVID. *(S.L. of her, looking front)* Wherever you say. Where would you like to go?

WANDA. Where would *you* like to go?

DAVID. I don't know any place. Do you?

WANDA. No. I've never been — you know — any place.

DAVID. Neither have I.

WANDA. *(pause)* You know my friend, Marge?

DAVID. What?

WANDA. Marge Baker?

DAVID. What about her?

WANDA. Well, she just happened to mention once that little park in back of the church on Elizabeth Street. She said it was very quiet there, and kind of romantic—

DAVID. *(pause)* Well, okay — except, I don't know —

WANDA. What?

DAVID. Back of the church — after all, we're both Jewish.

WANDA. If you'd rather not—

DAVID. Well, lets take a walk there, anyway.

(He takes her hand and they exit.)

ACT TWO

Scene 2

DAVID and WANDA enter through iron gates on platform. He leads her by the hand. They are in the cemetery. It is night.

WANDA. *(a little frightened)* I think we must be in the wrong place, David. Marge said a park. This is a cemetery. Let's go, Dave. Please.

DAVID. Maybe there's a park or something farther on. Let's just see where this leads.

WANDA. I don't think we should stay here. Please.

DAVID. *(at S.R., looking at footlights)* Wait a minute. It's not like a real cemetery. It's more like a museum. Look at this — "Agnes Beecher Thall — 1722 dash 1748 — Gentle soul, farewell!" They lived before the Revolution, Wanda!

WANDA. It's still a cemetery.

DAVID. *(He becomes more enthusiastic as he discovers more headstones. Crosses L. a few steps.)* Look at this one! "Henry Bascomb. 1719 dash 1764. Our village is a poorer place, our heaven a richer."

WANDA. *(S.R. of him)* That's beautiful.

74

DAVID. *(crossing L. to C.S.; squatting)* Must have been a nice man. And Wanda, look at this — "Emily and Joseph Weeks—"

WANDA. *(She squats beside him. Reads.)* "Did lie together as man and wife but for a moment. But shall lie under the stars for Eternity!" *(her hand on his arm)* That's beautiful.

DAVID. Shall we keep Mr. and Mrs Weeks company?

WANDA. *(gently)* All right.

(They rise. He puts boxes S.L. of him, takes off his jacket and spreads it for her.)

WANDA. *(She kneels on it, facing front, looking up at him.)* Maybe I should wear it. I feel a little chilly.

DAVID. Wait a minute. *(Opens package and puts his dinner jacket on her.)* Nice and comfortable? *(Kneels S.L. of her, facing her.)* But it's a shame to cover that beautiful dress of yours.

WANDA. David — I'm glad I told you why I wore this dress. I suppose I should feel ashamed — but I don't.

DAVID. Why should you? That's probably just how Emily won Joseph Weeks.

WANDA. I love you, David—

DAVID. *(He kisses her.)* I love you, Wanda. *(He kisses her again, a long, lingering kiss, then slips the coat from her shoulders, kisses her.*

(They look at each other.)

DAVID. You know what I think, Wanda?

WANDA. What, David?

DAVID. I think I better take you home. *(Picks up coat, puts it in box, then picks up boxes.)*

WANDA. *(after a pause)* All right — *(Rises and picks up jacket.)* But why?

DAVID. Well — I think that's the way Mr. and Mrs. Weeks would have wanted it. *(Puts his jacket around her. He moves to U.S. of her. Puts arm around her shoulders.)*

(They cross to gates and kiss. Lights dim out as they exit.)

LIGHTS FADE DOWN

ACT TWO

Scene 3

Scene: Kitchen. Early morning. Mother, in apron at stove, preparing breakfast.

MOTHER. *(spreading tablecloth)* Morris! It's almost half past! Breakfast!

FATHER. *(Enters from upstage, L. of C. wall, buttoning his shirt.)* All right, all right!

MOTHER. *(Getting spoons from table drawer, puts them on table.)* Morris, I have to talk to you. It's important.

FATHER. *(tucking his shirt into his pants and putting up suspenders)* Tonight.

MOTHER. Not tonight, now. Before you go to work. I don't like what's happening to David.

FATHER. What? What's happening?

MOTHER. Again he didn't come home till after three o'clock. And did you hear him? The way he snuck into the house, like a burglar?

FATHER. Three o'clock in the morning. Did you want him to sing the "Star Spangled Banner"?

MOTHER. He has new friends, Morris. Actors. *(taking handkerchief from apron pocket.)* Look what I picked up — lipstick on his handkerchief.

FATHER. Emma, you're worrying about nothing. Let me get dressed.

MOTHER. *(dishing up cerial from the stove)* Get dressed, then we'll talk.

(He exits, U.S.)

MOTHER. Two minutes you can spare for your son. *(Calls U.R.)* David, it's late.

(FATHER enters with necktie.)

DAVID. *(off)* Yes, Mother dear!

MOTHER. *(upset)* You hear him. "Yes, Mother dear!" Morris, I'm worried!

FATHER. *(Crosses D.S.R. and sits S.R. tieing necktie.)* Maybe this acting is only a stage — like model airplanes.

MOTHER. On his model airplanes, I didn't find lipstick! Morris, I've been thinking —

(Phone rings.)

MOTHER. At half-past seven? Who is it?

(Phone rings.)

MOTHER. Who could it be? *(Puts bowl of cereal at S.R. on table.)*

FATHER. *(Rises, crosses D.S. to U.L.)* I'll ask them.

(Phone rings. DAVID enters from U.R. of C. wall, sits R. of table ,

starts eating FATHER'S cereal. DAVID'S shirt is draped over his shoulders.)

FATHER. *(on phone)* Hello? ... Who? ... Yes, this is the Kolowitz residence.... It's for you, David. *(Puts phone down, crosses back to R. of table.)*

DAVID. *(rising, crossing L., below table, to phone)* Thanks—

MOTHER. *(worried)* At half-past seven? New friends, actors.

FATHER. *(crossing R., below table)* It was a girl.

MOTHER. *(worried)* Morris, talk to him. *(Crosses to DAVID.)*

FATHER. *(sitting S.R. of table)* Someone ate my farina.

DAVID. *(on phone, toward MOTHER)* Hello.... Hello, Wanda.

MOTHER. *(relieved)* Oh, it's Wanda. I'll get you more. *(Gets pot from stove. Dishes out more cereal for FATHER.)*

DAVID. Sure.... Sure I do.... Very much.... But gee, Wanda, it's half-past seven and ... okay ... *(Looks towards parents, surreptitiously kisses on phone.)* Tell you what, let's have lunch. Why don't you pick me up at my shop. 'Bye. *(Hangs up.)*

MOTHER. *(Puts pot on stove.)* David, get washed, and put on a clean shirt.

DAVID. *(Crosses D.S. and out U.R. of C. wall, kidding her.)* Very well, Mother dear! *(He exits.)*

MOTHER. *(She stares after him.)* Did you hear him!?

FATHER. All right, Emma. You want to tell me something. Tell me. I have to go to work.

MOTHER. Morris, sit down.

FATHER. I'm sitting.

MOTHER. *(Sits on stool, U.S, of table.)* Morris, I think we should borrow from Harry to send David to pharmacy school right now. What do you say?

FATHER. *(Rises, crosses U.R.)* I say no.

MOTHER. Why not?

FATHER. *(Crosses D. to chair.)* I don't want to borrow, especially from Harry. I needed a hernia operation, did I go runing to him? No, I managed.

MOTHER. You managed! You still need the hernia operation.

FATHER. I got a truss.

MOTHER. Congratulations.

FATHER. *(Crosses D.S.L. of table and crosses U.L., then D.L. of table.)* What's such an emergency you have to go running to Harry? The boy isn't in trouble; he wasn't arrested.

MOTHER. You want to wait until he's in trouble? You like his boss should call up that he's going to lose his job? You want to stay up worrying every night?

FATHER. So this is the emergency you want to run to Harry?

MOTHER. Yes. My boy is an emergency.

FATHER. My hernia's not an emergency?

MOTHER. You got a truss.

FATHER. Thank you. *(Crosses R. below table, then to U.R., then D. to R. of table.)*

MOTHER. Morris, listen to me — a sickness, the sooner you stop it, the better. Look how he changed in two days. "Yes, Mother dear!"

FATHER. *(Crosses L. below table to phone.)* All right. Maybe you're right.

MOTHER. Where are you going?

FATHER. *(He picks up phone, lifts receiver.)* I'll call up Harry.

MOTHER. Don't call him!

FATHER. Why not?

MOTHER. Because I did already.

FATHER. *(He hangs up, puts phone down, irritated. Crosses D.S. to chair, L. of table.)* You called him without asking me?

MOTHER. I told him I was going to ask you — I didn't want you to call him if he was going to say no.

FATHER. What did he say?

MOTHER. He said yes. He said he'd be glad to help. *(Puts cereal bowl from S.R. to S.L. on table.)*

FATHER. *(Sits L. of table.)* All right then, it's settled.

(DAVID enters, with two packages, on way out.)

MOTHER. *(rising)* David, where you running? Eat your breakfast.

DAVID. *(at door)* I'll be late. I must away.

MOTHER. If you went to sleep on time, you'd get up on time. Three o'clock. A boy should get at least eight hours sleep — a week! *(Turns U.S. to stove, stirs cereal.)*

DAVID. I told you why I was late. I had to rehearse. *(Takes actor pose.)*

MOTHER. Rehearsing what? I'll tell you what you're rehearsing. You're rehearsing for the cemetery. *(Dishes up cereal. Places it on S.R. of table.)*

DAVID. Ma, please let me get to — *(reacts)* What? What cemetery?

MOTHER. No sleep. Eating junk in restaurants — eat your breakfast.

DAVID. *(Crosses L., to her.)* My employer gets distraught if I am tardy.

MOTHER. *(Looks at FATHER.)* Maybe you won't be employed any more. *(Pours glass of orange juice.)*

DAVID. What do you mean?

FATHER. David, your boss telephoned us.

DAVID. *(Sits S.R. of table.)* Mr. Foreman? What did he want?

FATHER. He called like a friend. He said you were coming late, going early; he wanted to tell us like a friend.

DAVID. He fired me like a friend?

MOTHER. *(putting glass of orange juice at DAVID'S place, S.R. on table)* He didn't fire. But he warned.

DAVID. Okay. Then let me get to work, so I won't be late. I've got a big day.

MOTHER. *(Sits U.S. of table, on stool.)* What's the big day?

DAVID. You know, Ma. The show. Tonight.

MOTHER. There's not going to be any show for you tonight.

DAVID. I don't know what you're talking about. *(rising)* I bought my costume. Everything. It's the Marlowe Theatre on 18th Street. I want you to come and see me. Goodbye. *(Starts to door.)*

MOTHER. David—

DAVID. *(Stops at door, S.R.)* What?

MOTHER. *(rising)* We're registering you for pharmacy school, starting right away.

DAVID. *(crossing to R. of chair, R. of table)* What? What did you do that for? Who asked you to do that? Where'd you get the money?

FATHER. From your Uncle Harry.

DAVID. Uncle Harry? You haven't talked to Uncle Harry in a hundred years. Who asked you to do that?

MOTHER. Nobody asked us. We just decided.

DAVID. You decided? Why? What's the emergency?

FATHER. Our son is an emergency.

MOTHER. David, you're going to pharmacy school. And no more acting!

DAVID. What? I got to. They're depending on me. The show must go on.

MOTHER. And your mother and father? They don't have to go on?

DAVID. What are you talking about?

MOTHER. What am I talking about? Did you hear him, Morris? What am I talking about? A boy doesn't care that his mother is up a whole night, crying. *(Picks up his bowl, juice glass and spoon.)*

DAVID. Listen — I'm going to be an actor. I'm not going to be a druggist. I hate druggists!

MOTHER. *(Slams bowl, glass and spoon on to table, then speaks. The martyr.)* David, you do whatever you want. Don't worry how we feel, because our feelings don't matter. So do whatever you want, and forget about us. Papa and me don't matter.

(DAVID looks after her, distressed.)

FATHER. See what you're doing to Mama.

DAVID. Okay, okay, I'll be a druggist. I'll be a druggist, okay?

MOTHER. Whatever you want.

DAVID. *(Puts boxes on S.R. chair.)* Here's my costume. I can't go on without it. You happy now?

FATHER. I'm happy.

DAVID. You happy now?

MOTHER. We don't matter.

DAVID. Goodbye.

FATHER. Goodbye.

DAVID. *(to her)* Goodbye.

MOTHER. Whatever you want.

(DAVID exits.)

FATHER. He feels bad—

MOTHER. *(Puts cereal bowl and spoon on stove; folding tablecloth, putting it on stove.)* So he'll feel bad for a day, two days, a week — for the rest of his life he'll feel good.

FATHER. I'm going to work.

MOTHER. *(Puts packages on table, opens suit box, then the shawl box.)* Go to work. Nice material. What's this? A full dress suit, a top hat — and a prayer shawl. What kind of part is it? Maybe a reformed Rabbi?

ACT TWO

Scene 4

Scene: The shop. The following morning. FOREMAN is singing to himself as he works.

FOREMAN. It's up to *you* to do the hot-cha-cha.... It's up to you to do the hot-cha-cha....

(DAVID enters, pushes S.L. wall, changing it from kitchen to shop. FOREMAN looks at him. DAVID takes off jacket and hangs it up on hook on S.L. wall.)

FOREMAN. Ah, Mr. Barrymore is here! Good morning, Mr. Barrymore! *(Takes machine and tray of files from U.S. bench to D.S. table, then sits and works.)*

DAVID. Good morning.

FOREMAN. It's up to you to do the hot-cha-cha—

DAVID. Mr. Foreman, why did you have to call up my father?

FOREMAN. *(pause, then sings)* It's up to you to do the hot-cha-cha.... *(pause)* Why did I call up your father? Because if I had a boy, and my boy started acting foolish, started running around the street without his pants on, I would appreciate it if someone spent a nickle and telephoned me.

DAVID. *(at S.L.)* I didn't run around the street without my pants on.

FOREMAN. There are other ways to act foolish. *(works, sings)* It's up to you to do the hot-cha-cha—

DAVID. Did you tell my parents you were firing me?

FOREMAN. I told them, if!

DAVID. *(sitting L. of table)* If?

FOREMAN. If you come late, and leave early, and don't want to work, and don't want to learn, then yes. If not, then not! Everything, David, is if! Like the song says, David. It's up to you if you want to do the hot-cha-cha!

DAVID. *(half to self)* I don't want to do the hot-cha-cha....

FOREMAN. *(seriously)* What have I got here, David? A big factory with fifty machines? A small shop, but I make a living. Apples on the street, I don't sell. A son I don't have. A daughter I got, she's married with two children. Also girls. All right, girls have to live too. My daughter's husband, you met him, he talks nice, but he's a nebbish, he can do absolutely nothing, so he sells insurance. You know how much fire insurance I have for this shop? More than the Woolworth Building! So what's going to be with the shop? In case there's no fire! I have a helper. A good boy, handy, honest — so I teach him the trade — if he likes it, if he learns, who knows? With a younger person here, it could be a good business, who knows? Then what happens to this boy? All of a sudden, in one minute, he turns himself upside down, he turns himself inside out, he is doing the hot-cha-cha.

(DAVID doesn't answer. There is a pause.)

FOREMAN. Sure, I called your parents. If I didn't care, I wouldn't call. I wouldn't waste a nickle. But if your parents don't know what's what, they should know. You should have heard your mother. She cried on the telephone. She cried.

DAVID. *(doubts this)* My mother cried?

FOREMAN. And if she didn't cry? So what? I know a mother's heart. She felt like crying.

DAVID. Mr. Foreman, I'm not going to be in the play. I'm not going to act!

FOREMAN. *(He sits for a moment, rises and takes off apron.)* I have to see Mr. Reuben at Paris Bonnets... *(Hangs up apron on rack S.L. of C. wall shelves, takes hat and coat.)* I'll come back after lunch. *(Crosses to dor, opens it.)* You're a good boy! *(Exits.)*

DAVID. I trust I haven't kept you waiting too long, but I know that in your grief— *(He rises to U.S.C., picks up piece of machinery, works on it with file.)* Ah, the hell with it! *(shrugs, unhappily)*

(MARVIN enters, dressed in a neat brown suit. He moves S.L. chair to U.S.L. and sits.)

MARVIN. Tonight's the big night, eh, Dave?

DAVID. *(U.R. of table)* Is that why you came to work all dressed up?

MARVIN. Yeah, I figured I'd eat in a cafeteria, instead of going home, so I'd be sure to be on time. *(Fixes crease in pants.)*

DAVID. Well, you can go home after work, Marve. I'm not going to be in the play.

MARVIN. Why? What happened? Were you canned?

DAVID. No, nothing like that.

MARVIN. Does Wanda know?

DAVID. Yeah, I called her.

MARVIN. Gee, don't tell me that you're scared to be in it?

DAVID. No, of course not. It's just that my mother and father don't want me to do it.

MARVIN. Oh, them!

DAVID. *(stops working)* What do you mean, oh them?

MARVIN. I mean — well, you know — *parents!*

DAVID. What do you mean, parents?

MARVIN. Gee, Dave, I got nothing against your mother and father. I didn't mean it that way.

DAVID. *(Tosses tools into tray on table.)* Well, what way did you mean it?

MARVIN. *(Rises, crosses R.)* All I meant was— I don't get you, Dave. What are you getting so hot about?

DAVID. *(Crosses to upstage of table.)* I'll tell you what I'm getting so hot about. A guy does something because his mother and father ask him to, and all of a sudden he's a criminal or something. That's what I'm getting so hot about!

MARVIN. *(Crosses to DAVID.)* But I thought you wanted to be in the play. You wanted to be an actor.

DAVID. Of course I did!

MARVIN. That's all I meant.

DAVID. *(Crosses D.S.R. off platform.)* Ah, shut up!

(WANDA enters, crosses R. below to S.L. of DAVID, putting purse on table as she crosses.)

DAVID. Hello, Wanda.

WANDA. Hello, David. Hello, Marvin.

MARVIN. Hi.

(She goes to DAVID, uncertain what to do. They turn and look at MARVIN.)

DAVID. *(to MARVIN)* Won't your boss be sore that you're out so long?

MARVIN. *(at U.R. of table)* Let him be sore! *(pause)* You want me to get out of here?

DAVID. You can go or stay. Do whatever you want!

MARVIN. *(crossing toward door, U.L.)* Okay, if that's how you feel! *(He walks towards door, but sits in chair near door.)*

(DAVID crosses U.S.C.)

WANDA. *(Crosses L. to DAVID.)* What happened, David? What did you mean, you're not going to act in the play tonight?

DAVID. Well, it's kind of complicated—

MARVIN. His parents don't want him to!

WANDA. Is that why, David?

DAVID. Yes, but they've got their reasons.

WANDA. *(Shakes head.)* Parents! *(Crosses R. a few steps.)*

MARVIN. *(kidding)* What do you mean, parents?

DAVID. *(U.L.of table)* Just shut up, Marv. Just keep quiet and shut up!

MARVIN. *(Rises to S.L. of DAVID.)* What are you sore at me for? If you're sore at them, what are you taking it out on me for?

WANDA. *(S.R. of DAVID)* What kind of reasons do they have?

DAVID. They're mad because I've been coming home so late. Like last night.

WANDA. But last night wasn't because of them.

DAVID. I know. But I couldn't tell them where I really was, could I?

MARVIN. *(S.L. of DAVID)* Why? Where were you last night?

(DAVID crosses L. below table to S.L. WANDA follows him.)

DAVID. Anyway, I promised them I won't be in the play tonight. So that's the way it is.

MARVIN. *(following to below table)* Why is that the way it is? That doesn't have to be the way it is. You know what you can do. I'll tell you what you can do.

DAVID. All right, tell me. What can I do?

MARVIN. Don't tell them. That's what you can do. Do the play and tell them something else.

(DAVID crosses R. above table, U.S. then to D.R.)

MARVIN. Tell them you got a date with me, or with Wanda — like last night — Hey, where'd you guys go last night? *(Sits C. on table, facing front.)*

DAVID. *(D.R.)* They made me promise. It's important to them.

WANDA. *(D.L. of table)* Why is it so important to them? What's so terrible if you act in a play?

DAVID. *(Crosses U.S. and D.S. again.)* You know what they

did, Wanda? They borrowed money from my Uncle Harry so I could take up pharmacy.

WANDA. They did? That's wonderful.

DAVID. *(at D.R.)* They want me to start pharmacy school right away, and quit the play.

WANDA. Maybe if you told them it's just for a few nights, ... you can still go to pharmacy school—

DAVID. *(Crosses to S.R. of table.)* What do you mean, a few nights? If I'm marvelous, they'd keep me.

WANDA. *(D.L. of table)* So?

DAVID. So? I don't understand you, Wanda. I can't be everything, a druggist — a machinist — an actor—

MARVIN. After all, he's only one person.

DAVID. Shut up! *(Crosses R. and turns; speaks.)* After all, Wanda, I'm only one person — I have to give up the play.

WANDA. Well — if you really have to—

DAVID. *(surprised)* Don't you mind that I'm giving up the play?

WANDA. Sure I do. In a way. Acting in the play for a few nights would be very interesting. But I didn't think you meant to throw everything away.

DAVID. *(D.R.)* What do you mean, "throw away?" What have I got to throw away?

WANDA. *(Crosses R. to DAVID.)* Well, I mean college; your work. After all, you can't depend on acting; they're not even paying you. How are you going to support anybody?

DAVID. *(Crosses D.L., below table.)* Who do I have to support? I have no wife, I have no kids. You know, Wanda, you're beginning to sound exactly like my mother.

WANDA. David, I didn't come here to be insulted.

DAVID. *(Crosses R. to L. of table.)* What did you come here for? To tell me what I can do and what I can't do?

WANDA. *(Crosses L. to D.R. of table.)* Somebody better tell you. You're acting like a child.

DAVID. I am, huh? Wanda, I'll do anything I want.

MARVIN. I think you're right, Dave.

DAVID. Shut up. *(to WANDA)* I bet you're sorry now you lent me that ten dollars.

WANDA. Maybe I am. If you're going to be like this about it.

DAVID. I wish I could give it back. Right now.

WANDA. *(Crosses D.S.L. to DAVID.)* I don't care about the money. I care about you.

DAVID. Sure. Sure you do.

MARVIN. If you really cared about him—

WANDA. *(viciously)* You shut up!

DAVID. *(to WANDA)* Don't worry about the money. You'll get it.

WANDA. *(angry)* All right! If you haven't got the money, I'll take the suit.

DAVID. I haven't got it. It's home. And you know something else? I'm going to be in the play. I don't care what you or anybody thinks. I'm going to do what I want.

WANDA. You don't care what I think?

DAVID. No! Not if you're going to be that way — no, I don't.

(WANDA crosses U.L. and out. DAVID crosses R. to D.R. She returns for bag. MARVIN hands bag to WANDA and she exits again.)

MARVIN. *(Rises, crosses L. around table to U.L. of it.)* Hey, what did you guys do last night?

DAVID. *(Crosses L. to MARVIN.)* Ooh. Marvin ... listen ... will you do me a favor?

MARVIN. Yeah.

DAVID. Will you go to my house and ask my sister to give you the white box in my room?

MARVIN. Yeah.

DAVID. And bring it to the theatre. Okay?

MARVIN. *(exiting)* Yeah. Great, Dave.

DAVID. *(exiting after taking jacket from hook)* Whee!

(MARVIN exits upstage. DAVID exits off L, above second portal. Turntable goes counterclockwise to DAVID'S dressing room.)

ACT TWO

Scene 5

Dressing room. It is empty at rise.

PIKE. *(Entering from L. above first portal, crosses stage.)* This way, Colman. This way.

(DAVID follows from above second portal. PIKE opens door, steps to S.R. of it. DAVID crosses to above dressing table.)

PIKE. Here's your dressing room. There's some make-up for you.

DAVID. Make-up? You mean for my face?

PIKE. Well — if you want to put it any place else, that's your business. Where's your costume?

DAVID. *(Takes stool from S.R. of table and puts it U.S. of table.)* A friend is bringing it — did he come yet?

PIKE. No one came.

DAVID. Oh, would you please make sure to let him in? His name is Marvin.

PIKE. I don't care what his name is. I'll let him in. We let anybody in. *(exits)*

DAVID. *(Hangs up jacket on clothes tree U.S. of dressing table.)* I trust I haven't kept you waiting too long, but I know that in your grief, time had no meaning.... What the hell does that mean? ... I trust I haven't kept you waiting too long —

(Door opens, and MARVIN enters. He is carrying a package.)

DAVID. Marvin! You're late. *(Takes package from him, puts it on table.)*

MARVIN. I had to wait until your mother didn't see me.

DAVID. *(taking off tie and hanging it on clothes tree)* You better go out and get a seat. They're starting soon.

MARVIN. How much is a ticket?

DAVID. It's free.

MARVIN. Free?

DAVID. Just tell them you're a friend of mine. And later, when they take up a collection, you don't have to give anything.

MARVIN. They take up a collection?

DAVID. For the scenery. They do that in all the big Broadway shows.

MARVIN. Good luck, Dave.

DAVID. Thank you.

(MARVIN exits.)

DAVID. *(Looks in box, pulls out prayer shawl. Calls:)* Marvin!

MARVIN. *(re-entering)* What?

DAVID. *(in a panic)* Where's the suit? You didn't bring the suit.

MARVIN. What suit? You told me to bring the package. I didn't look in it.

DAVID. *(Puts prayer shawl box on steamer chair, D.R.)* What am I going to do? I can't wear this. What am I going to do?

MARVIN. I'm sorry, David, I only—

DAVID. Go out and find Mr. Marlowe.

MARVIN. Who?

DAVID. Mr. Marlowe. Ask everybody if he is Mr. Marlowe.

(MARVIN exits. DAVID talks to himself. There is a knock on the door.)

DAVID. Oh, Mr. Marlowe, I—

MISS B. *(Enters in evening gown.)* Hello, David.

DAVID. Miss B. Laura. What are you doing here? I thought you couldn't come.

MISS B. I can't. I mean, I can't stay. But I thought I'd just drop by, at least to wish you luck. Good luck, David, in the play tonight. *(She shakes hands with him.)* I must run, David, there's a cab waiting—

DAVID. I can't be in it.

MISS B. Why? What's the matter?

DAVID. I don't have my tuxedo. I have it, but it's at home.

MISS B. You mean, if you don't have a dress suit, you can't act tonight?

DAVID. *(nods)* That's right.

MISS B. Wait! Wait here! *(She exits.)*

DAVID. *(U.S. of dressing table)* Where would I go? What

am I going to do? I know what I'm going to do, I'm going to kill myself, that's what I'm going to do.

(MISS B. re-enters, holding ROGER by the hand. He is wearing a tuxedo. As soon as he enters, DAVID stares at the suit with envy. ROGER is unhappy about the whole thing.)

ROGER. *(as she opens door and leads him in by hand)* This is absurd, ridiculous. Let's get out of here, Laura. We'll be late, Laura.

(MISS B. crosses to D.R. of platform. ROGER crosses down to her, S.L.)

MISS B. What if we are a little late? What does it matter? David, this is my gentleman friend, Roger. This is David, Roger, the boy I told you about.

ROGER. How are you, fella? It's ridiculous, Laura. *(pulling hand away from DAVID)* Why should I lend him my suit? We'll be hours late. The banquet is for nine o'clock.

MISS B. What if we are late? We'll just miss a bunch of silly speeches about hats.

ROGER. Laura, my boss will be there!

MISS B. You can tell your boss what happened; he might think it's funny.

ROGER. What's funny about it? I don't see anything funny. Come on Laura. *(crossing up to door)* Are you coming or aren't you?

MISS B. No. If you're going to be that way, I'm not coming.

(ROGER stands by door, unbelieving.)

Miss B. I don't care about your old banquet, anyway. I'm just surprised at you, Roger Finestein. I thought you were a different type of person, with some consideration. So have a good time at your banquet and I'll stay here and watch David in his play. *(Turns away, D.R.)*

David. I can't be in it.

Roger. *(Crosses down to her.)* What's consideration got to do with anything? *(Crosses to DAVID.)*

(DAVID sits on stool.)

Roger. Who says I'm not considerate? I'm considerate. Ask my mother. Ask her if I don't give thirty bucks into the house every week, rain or shine, and I eat home only maybe once, twice a week for my thirty bucks. Who says I'm not considerate? *(crossing to her, S.L.)* What do you care about this kid? Who is he, anyway?

Miss B. That's not the point.

Roger. What's the point? Tell me that. What is the point that's so important I have to go to a banquet in my underwear?

Miss B. The point is, I thought you were the sort of person who would make a sacrifice for someone else.

Roger. *(Crosses R. to her.)* I do, I do. I give plenty. I give to all the diseases.

Miss B. I'll tell you the truth, Roger. I was seriously considering that I would say yes if you asked, you know, the question. Because of the type of person I thought you were. Now I don't know.

ROGER. I am that type.

MISS B. I'm not so sure.

ROGER. You mean if I lend this kid my suit, you'd marry me? Is that what you mean? It really means that much to you?

MISS B. I really does. Because of what it shows about you as a person.

ROGER. Okay. Okay. *(Jacket off, tosses it on steamer chair.)* What the hell. You only live once. *(Trousers off, gives them to DAVID, crosses L., then back to D.R. of set.)*

DAVID. *(rising)* Gee, thanks very much, Laura. Thank you sir....

MISS B. *(crossing up to door)* Of course. I'll get right out. We'll go to the banquet right after the play. Good luck, David. *(Crosses to ROGER, kisses cheek.)* And, Rog, you're a real darling. Honestly. *(Crosses up to door.)* We'll laugh about this on our honeymoon. *(as she exits:)* I can't believe it! I did it!

(DAVID takes pants off, hangs them on clothes tree, then takes off shirt and hangs it up.)

ROGER. *(bewildered, crossing up to DAVID)* Yeah, sure. This is sure one for the books. I sure hope my boss appreciates the joke, when I barge in two hours late. *(Takes off tie, puts it on steamer chair, and notices prayer shawl.)* What's this doing here?

DAVID. *(putting on pants)* It's mine.

ROGER. *(Picks up shawl from chair, crosses to S.R. of DAVID.)* You bring this every place? What are you, a religious fanatic or something?

DAVID. *(Taking box, putting lid on it, and puts it in U.L. corner of the room.)* No, my friend brought it instead of the suit.

ROGER. How could he mix this up with a suit?

DAVID. Well—

ROGER. Ah, forget it. *(Crosses R.)* This whole thing is crazy. *(taking off shirt)* You know what the craziest thing of all is? I'll tell you what the craziest thing of all is. On account of I'm lending you my suit, Laura's going to marry me. That's crazy, right? *(Gives shirt to DAVID.)*

DAVID. I guess so. *(Puts on dress shirt.)*

ROGER. *(crossing D.S.)* You know what's even crazier? I don't want to get married! *(Crosses U.S. to DAVID.)* And now I'm engaged. I mean, I figured maybe sometime. *(Crosses D.R. again.)* But here I am, as soon as I take off my pants, I'm engaged all of a sudden. *(crossing up to DAVID)* She does expect me to marry her, right?

DAVID. I think so.

ROGER. *(crossing R. a few steps)* Who wants to get married? I mean now. *(Sits in steamer chair.)* In the middle of the season. But what the hell, I could do worse, right? Laura's a nice kid, right?

DAVID. *(U.S. of table)* She's very nice.

ROGER. *(rising, suspicious)* What do you know about her? *(Crosses U.S. to him.)* How do you know how nice she is? I mean, how well do you know her?

DAVID. I just deliver to her place. Sewing machines.

ROGER. Oh. She's a good kid. And built! Right?

ROGER. Yes.

ROGER. I could do worse! You don't need my shoes, do you?

DAVID. No thanks.

ROGER. *(Helps DAVID with collar and tie, taking him D.R.S. off platform.)* This sure is funnier than a barrel of monkeys. My suit acting on the stage; how about that! I never done any acting myself — but I've always been interested. The fact is, my line of work is seventy-five percent acting, too. A little personality, a couple risky stories, throw the crap around. Same as acting, right? Don't get any stains on this, will you? *(Stands behind DAVID with arms around his neck, fixing tie.)*

MARLOWE. *(Enters, crosses to D.C.)* What's the matter, Don? Hasn't your suit—? *(stopped by what he sees)* We don't go for this sort of thing!

ROGER. *(turning to MARLOWE)* Who's he?

DAVID. *(at S.R. of ROGER)* Mr. Marlowe, I haven't got my suit for the play, and this man's lending me his.

MARLOWE. *(bewildered)* He is?

DAVID. Yes, sir. He's a friend of mine. *(Gets coat from steamer chair.)*

MARLOWE. He must be. *(He exits.)*

DAVID. *(reciting)* "It's good to find one human being in this ridiculous place."

ROGER. Forget the compliments. Just don't wrinkle the suit.

DAVID. *(Crosses U.S., putting on coat.)* You want to put on my clothes and watch the show?

ROGER. *(Takes newspaper from behind wooden cross-piece upstage of steamer chair.)* No, I think I'll stay here and take a nap. It's going to be a long night. *(Sits on steamer chair, puts blanket from arm of chair over his legs.)* Good luck, kid. *(Reads paper.)*

DAVID. *(at U.S. of table)* Thanks. Thanks very much. "I

trust I haven't kept you waiting too long, but I know that in your grief time had no meaning—"

ROGER. *(Sits up.)* What? What's that you said?

DAVID. It's from the play. It's my first lines.

ROGER. Oh. Okay. *(Sits back.)*

(DAVID continues dressing, mumbling lines to himself. WANDA enters, carrying a package. Her maner is remote and restrained.)

WANDA. *(C.)* David? *(belligerently)* Here's your suit.

DAVID. *(He takes package from her, puts it on table.)* Oh — how did you get it?

WANDA. From your house. Where did you get that one?

DAVID. *(indicating ROGER)* From him. He lent it to me. But thanks for bringing it.

WANDA. Well — you're welcome. *(Starts out.)*

PIKE. *(calling from off L.)* Three minutes, Colman!

DAVID. *(calls)* Okay! Wanda, are you going to watch the play?

WANDA. Well — do you want me to?

DAVID. Yes, sure I do.

WANDA. Then I will. Good luck, David. *(Shakes hands with him, then impulsively, they hug. Then to ROGER.)* Good bye, sir. Nice to have met you. *(She exits.)*

ROGER. *(Was reading, sits up abruptly.)* What? Who was that?

DAVID. "I trust I haven't kept—"

(MOTHER enters, followed by FATHER. They come from upstage of second portal, S.R.)

DAVID. Ma. Pa. What are you doing here?

(MOTHER is at S.L of door. FATHER is S.R. of her.)

MOTHER. David, if Marvin sneaks out with a package and Wanda sneaks out with a package, what should we think?

DAVID. Do me a favor. Don't say anything now. Watch the show and we'll talk about it later.

PIKE. *(offstage)* Hurry up, Colman.

DAVID. I'll be right out.

MOTHER. *(indicating ROGER)* Who's he? Another actor?

DAVID. Him? No, he's a hat salesman.

ACT TWO

Scene 6

Small stage and section of offstage. The offstage section, U.S.L. consists of the stage manager's ledge. PIKE is standing there, looking onstage. Onstage is the set of what is meant to be a sumptuous living room, although it is meagerly and shabbily furnished. MARLOWE is standing U.R. of S.L. chair with back to audience. ANGELA is seated on love seat. A LAWYER is seated in chair D.R. and the two young DONS are onstage. The two DONS are sitting behind the couch, obviously uncomfortable and embarrassed. At rise, they are in the midst of the scene of the play. DON DARWIN U.S.L end love seat. DON BAXTER U.S.R. end love seat.

MARLOWE. *(turning to audience, crossing downstage of chair; to the lawyer)* But surely, Peabody, you can tell us something of the contents of poor Effingwell's will—

LAWYER. *(Seated D.R.)* I'm sorry, but I cannot disclose its contents until all the heirs are gathered.

MARLOWE. But good heavens, man — you know Jeff Heming. He may be anywhere, China, Australia, any where. That young scamp is thoroughly irresponsible. *(Sits.)*

ANGELA. *(Rises.)* Now, Horace, Jeff sent word that he

will be here this afternoon. He may be irresponsible, but he is a man of his word. *(Sits.)*

(pause)

PIKE. *(prompting)* I find this waiting and not knowing unbearable.

LAWYER and DON BAXTER. *(simultaneously, as they rise)* I find this waiting and not knowing— *(They turn and look at each other.)* unbearable—

(MARLOWE rises, stares at DON BAXTER, who sits down, miserably. LAWYER sits chair S.R.)

ANGELA. *(rising)* Well, shall I serve some tea? Perhaps it will make the waiting a little less unbearable. *(She begins to pour tea.)*

PIKE. *(at D.L. of set, calls U.S.)* Okay Colman, this is your cue coming. *(Rings doorbell mounted on board.)*

ANGELA. I imagine that's Jeff now. *(Crosses U.S. Looks at door, U.L.)*

(Actors look to door. DAVID crosses to PIKE. MOTHER and FATHER follow DAVID.)

DAVID. *(S.L. of PIKE)* Ma. Pa. You can watch from here—

PIKE. No, nobody stays here—

DAVID. They're my mother and father.

PIKE. Nobody stays here.

DAVID. Please.

PIKE. They can't stay.

DAVID. Then I'm not going on!

ANGELA. *(crossing D. to above coffee table)* Perhaps it was a peddler— or something— *(Starts pouring.)*

PIKE. They can go out front.

DAVID. No, it will be too late. They'll miss the whole thing.

PIKE. Okay, okay. Just get out there!

(PIKE pushes him U.S. and through U.C.S. doors of set. He is shoved onstage. He stumbles through doors to D.C. of set, shakes his fist at PIKE, then turns front, sees audience and freezes. PIKE crosses to D.L. of set again and rings bell.)

ANGELA. That's probably Jeff now.

MARLOWE. *(crossing D.S. to L. of DAVID)* I suppose, knowing you, Jeff, that you trust you haven't kept us waiting too long—

DAVID. *(mouthing words)* I trust I haven't kept you waiting too long....

(DAVID moves his lips but no sound emerges. MARLOWE looks closely at his mouth, then puts his ear to DAVID'S mouth, then straightens up. DAVID, still trying to talk, puts his hand on his lapel, MARLOWE removes it. He then clutches MARLOWE who takes his hand away. DAVID slowly raises his right hand and MARLOWE slaps it down.)

MARLOWE. I beg your pardon?

DAVID. *(Blurts out loudly.)* But in my grief time had no meaning.

LAWYER. *(rising)* Why are you so late, Jeff?

DAVID. *(Weak chuckle, slightly under control now. Crossing R., below coffee table, to its R.)* Strange how suddenly I seem to be missed.

(LAWYER sits.)

MARLOWE. *(twirling sash of his robe)* You can only blame yourself, Jeff. You disappeared overnight without a trace.... Without a trace.

(a pause, as they wait for DAVID'S next line)

ANGELA. *(Leans over him, prompting him.)* That's not true, Horace....

DAVID. *(flinging his arm out, hitting ANGELA)* That's not true, Horace, and you know it.

ANGELA. Are you suggesting that Horace knew of your whereabouts?

DAVID. *(Wheels around, his arm extended, so that he almost hits her in the head.)* Yes. Ask him. *(Keeps arm extended.)*

MARLOWE. *(Lowers DAVID'S arm .... calmly)* If I may say a word....

ANGELA. Yes, Horace. Please do. *(Takes out cigarette.)*

DAVID. *(picking up matches)* Allow me. *(He lights a match, but neglects to light her cigarette.)* Go on, Horace, you were saying? *(He drops his hand with lit match.)*

(ANGELA follows the hand, bending down to get her cigarette lit.... She blows out match, during following speech.)

MARLOWE. Whether or not I knew of Jeff's whereabouts is of no consequence. It will in no way alter the terms of the will, which, I believe, leaves the estate to me. May we have it read, please?

LAWYER. Certainly, I....

DAVID. Before you open that envelope, there is in existence another document that may alter the terms of the will.

MARLOWE. I don't believe it.... You're lying!

DAVID. Am I? *(chuckles)* Let me get it and I'll be in a position to prove my point. *(He wheels quickly toward door, steps on ANGELA'S foot.*

ANGELA. *(Screeches in pain, quickly recovers.)* That's very interesting, Jeff.

DAVID. Excuse me, Angela.... *(Winces at his mistake.)* I mean, Harriet.... *(Takes a document out of briefcase.)*

FATHER. How do you like him?

MOTHER. He's the best one.

DAVID. *(brandishing document)* While you thought of me as a mere playboy, these last few years I have been on a secret mission for my uncle.

MARLOWE. He's lying.

ANGELA. Go on, Jeff.

DAVID. Thank you, my dear. As you will see, this document gives me complete control of my uncle's vast fortune. I assure you it will not be used *(extravagant sawing arm gestures)* for yachts ... or for gambling ... or for fancy women....

MARLOWE. Pretty words! And may I ask what plans you have for this fortune?

DAVID. To fulfill my uncle's dream and mine. This

money will be used to educate people of all nations and insure peace in the world forever.

ANGELA. Oh, Jeff!

(They embrace....and exit.)

MARLOWE. Fate .... is a strange mistress! *(Has sudden heart attack, collapses, dies.)*

(Blackout .... lights up .... They take bows....)

BLACKOUT

ACT TWO

Scene 7

Scene: The stage....

DON BAXTER and DON DARWIN. Very good, Colman.....
nice job....

DAVID. Thanks...

(As MARLOWE enters, with ANGELA:)

DAVID. Oh, Mr. Marlowe. I'm sorry about the beginning. I was a little nervous.

MARLOWE. My boy, I have seen many forms of stage-
fright in my time, but your entrance tonight was unique
and classic.

ANGELA. Nonsense, Don. You were splendid. In your
way. Wasn't he splendid, Daddy? In his way?

MARLOWE. Yes, splendid.... *(To self, as he starts off.)*
Where the hell is that bottle?

ANGELA. Don, I'm going to talk to Daddy about your
tuition.

DAVID. Oh, the three dollars.... Can I pay it next
week?

110

ANGELA. *(Shakes head.)* Don, I feel that, because you show such promising talent .... you should be allowed to act for nothing.... *(Kisses him on cheek.)* See you tomorrow, Don darling. *(Exits.)*

DAVID. *(thrilled)* Act for nothing! Wow!

(WANDA, MARVIN, MOTHER and FATHER enter.)

DAVID. Well, Wanda?

WANDA. You were wonderful, David.

DAVID. I loused up the first part.

MARVIN. You were great, Dave. Great acting. Great laughing. Great.

DAVID. Well, Ma, did you like it?

MOTHER. Yes, David. You were very nice.

DAVID. I'll be better tomorrow.... I like it, Ma. It's what I like.

MOTHER. But if it's a mistake?

DAVID. Then it's my mistake. Okay?

FATHER. We'll talk about it.

DAVID. Sure, but I'll talk too.... Okay, Ma?

MOTHER. *(Pats him on cheek, warmly.)* David, haven't I always said .... whatever you want!

FATHER. You were very good, David ... especially what you said about peace in the world.

PIKE. *(Enters, and crosses off.)* Everybody out!

DAVID. I'll meet you all outside, soon as I change.... We'll go someplace to eat.

(They start off.)

DAVID. Where do you want to go, Wanda? To a cafeteria, a delicatessen or what?

WANDA. Like your mother said .... whatever you want! *(Exits.)*

DAVID. *(Alone, looks around stage.) (simply)* Hello.... My name is David Kolowitz.... I'm an actor.

CURTAIN